Olive Oil *Desserts*

© 2008 MICKI'S KITCHEN

COVER PHOTOGRAPH BACIPHOTOGRAPHY.COM
EDITOR MEGAN MARTIN
BOOK DESIGN BY 📖 theBookDesigners

PUBLISHED IN THE UNITED STATES BY
MIKKO PUBLISHING
356 NORTH MEADOW LANE, D-9 #334
AMERICAN FORK, UTAH 84003

978-0-9801349-0-2

SANNAR, MICKI
OLIVE OIL DESSERTS / MICKI SANNAR
P. CM.
INCLUDES INDEX
COPYRIGHT TX-6-553-576

SANNAR, MICKI.
OLIVE OIL DESSERTS : DELICIOUS AND HEALTHY
HEART
SMART BAKING : RECIPES / BY MICKI SANNAR.
P. CM.
INCLUDES BIBLIOGRAPHICAL REFERENCES AND
INDEX.
LCCN 2007278394
ISBN-13: 978-0-9801349-0-2
ISBN-10: 0-9801349-0-0

1. COOKERY (OLIVE OIL) 2. DESSERTS. I. TITLE.

TX819.O42S355 2009   641.6'463
QBI08-600255

Olive Oil *Desserts*

DELICIOUS AND HEALTHY
HEART SMART BAKING

Recipes by

MICKI SANNAR

MIKKO PUBLISHING
HIGHLAND, UTAH

Table of *Contents*

ACKNOWLEDGMENTS

I WOULD LIKE TO EXPRESS MY APPRECIATION to the many people who have supported and helped me along the way. This unique cookbook was started over six years ago and I sometimes wondered if it would ever be completed. Many of my dear friends, family, and cooking students have been very patient and kind, waiting on this unique little cookbook.

Thank you to Angelique and her three sweet daughters, who were my original olive oil dessert guinea pigs. To Judy C. who was the right person at just the right time. To Annie for trying anything I sent her way and for sharing her kitchen. To Roni, who shared my ups and downs and encouraged me everyday. To my parents, Don and Estelle, who gave me a love of all types of food.

My thanks to Carol who gave me the push I needed to complete this project and for giving me the opportunity to show this special book to the people of Utah first. And thank you sweet Carrie for going the extra mile to help me in the final stages of the first edition of this cookbook!

A special thanks to my beautiful and talented children; Ryan, Christopher, Michael and my Angel Jessica. You have been my best cheerleaders. Thanks for helping out in the kitchen and bragging about my "amazing tasting desserts." Also, for eating dessert three or more times a day when all you really wanted by then was a nice green salad.

And to my darling husband David, he helped me to believe in myself more than I thought possible. I appreciate his wisdom, intelligence and his deep love for me. I love you sweetie!

There are so many people who have helped encourage me – you know who you are! Please know of my sincere gratitude.

And finally, I am grateful to my Father in Heaven who has blessed me with such a loving family and true friends, and enough treats to share with others.

LEARN THESE WARNING SIGNS AND ACT QUICKLY IF YOU SEE SOMEONE HAVING THEM.

Heart Attack Warning Signs
- Uncomfortable pressure, squeezing, fullness or pain in the center of the chest that lasts more than a few minutes or goes away and comes back.
- Pain or discomfort in one or both arms, the back, neck, jaw or stomach.
- Shortness of breath, with or without chest discomfort.
- Other signs such as breaking out in a cold sweat, nausea or lightheadedness.

Stroke Warning Signs
- Sudden numbness or weakness of the face, arm or leg, especially on one side of the body.
- Sudden confusion, trouble speaking or understanding.
- Sudden trouble seeing in one or both eyes.
- Sudden trouble walking, dizziness, loss of balance or coordination.
- Sudden, severe headache with no known cause.

Not all of these warning signs occur in every heart attack or stroke. If some start to occur, get help immediately. Heart attack and stroke are medical emergencies! Call 9-1-1.

(SOURCE: AMERICAN HEART ASSOCIATION)

The DISCOVERY

MORE THAN SIX YEARS AGO, through a routine physical examination both my husband (Dave) and I were told that we had elevated levels of LDL cholesterol. We have always tried to eat fresh and balanced home cooked meals and only occasionally eat fast food. However, upon learning about the damage LDL cholesterol can do to the heart, we began making more changes in our diet. The one thing that was a challenge to us was dessert. We are from a long line of dessert lovers, and I was well known around town as the dessert queen. I can cook just about anything; however, desserts are my favorite food group.

As I began looking for healthier ways to make my sweet treats, I discovered for myself the heart healthy benefits of olive oil. I was pleased to learn that not only is olive oil good for you, it's great for you! Of all the many different oils on the market today, olive oil is proven to be the most beneficial in helping to lower LDL (bad) cholesterol and to raise HDL (good) cholesterol. I felt like I had just won the lottery!!!

Next, I began searching for traditional dessert recipes that included olive oil. I couldn't find any and I wondered if I could replace the butter in my recipes and use olive oil instead. My first try, the traditional Chocolate Chip Cookie, came out too oily. The next step was to lower the amount of olive oil that I was using. What I discovered was that only about ⅔ of a cup of olive oil is needed to replace 1 cup of butter. I began experimenting and creating other desserts. The ⅔ cup to 1 cup ratio was not always a perfect match, so with a bit of adjusting in each recipe, I started seeing fantastic results! I was so pleased that I began conjuring up even more recipes. The taste and texture of each of these little confections was nothing short of amazing. I even figured out a way to convert many of my delicious treats into a whole grain version with impressive results (see page 25). The best thing about my sweet little discovery was that my family, friends and cooking students loved them. I was once again back in the dessert queen business! Only this time I had a healthier version of desserts that everyone was sure to love.

Over the past few years, unhealthy trans-fats and hydrogenated oils have been making headlines in major media outlets. Some states have even successfully banned the use of these unhealthy fats from public eating establishments. A few larger restaurant chains have started to boast that they are now trans fat free!

Many medical studies have been conducted on the health benefits of olive oil. These studies have scientifically proven that olive oil reduces bad cholesterol (LDL) and increases good cholesterol (HDL). In addition, there are many more health related benefits which come from using olive oil. (See page 17 to learn more).

The great news for both Dave and I was that when we started incorporating olive oil into our daily diet, we noticed a drop in our LDL cholesterol.

Thank you for purchasing "*Olive Oil Desserts,*" the very first cookbook of its kind! I know you will enjoy delighting your family and friends with these delicious, nearly guilt-free treats. Remember, life is short, enjoy dessert first (as long as it's made with olive oil!).

Happy Baking!
—*Micki Sannar*

Cooking is all about family and friends and there is joy found in cooking for others.

My Philosophy on Wealth:

If I have enough food to feed myself,
I am doing somewhat well.

If I have enough food to feed my family,
I am well off.

However, if I have enough food to feed others,
Especially those who visit my home,

I am wealthy!

The recipes in this cookbook were created and baked with love to share with family and friends. In my kitchen there is a sign on the wall that reads; "Cooking is Love Made Visible." Cooking and eating make up so much of our lives – I truly believe that a meal, especially a dessert tastes best when you share it with those you love.

Scattered throughout this cookbook, I have inserted among the recipes a few fun quotes and tips, as well as some cute cooking stories given to me by others, and there are a few of my own. Some stories may make you smile, some may make you laugh out loud, and some may bring back a sweet or funny memory you have made while cooking.

I hope you become very wealthy!

Happy Baking!

OLIVE OIL HAS BEEN CALLED "GOD'S ELIXIR." The Egyptians believe that the goddess Isis taught the people how to cultivate and use olives. Greek mythology tells of the goddess Athena who – by bestowing the olive tree upon mankind – won a competition between the gods over who could introduce the most useful gift to the people.

Although the origin of the first olive trees is unknown, olives have been cultivated since about 6000 B.C. We do know that it is one of the earliest noted plants in recorded history, and that the olive tree is indigenous to southern Asia Minor (modern day Syria and Palestine) where wild olive forests still exist. Olive trees live to a great age, with one tree in Crete dating back more than two thousand years.

Through trade, the Phoenicians brought the olive tree from Syria to Greece and Spain, and the Greeks are credited with introducing the olive tree to Rome. Through human cultivation, olive trees spread throughout the Mediterranean region where their fruit became a central part of these people's diet. It is believed that sometime around 2000 B.C. olive oil was first produced.

The first Olympic torch was said to be a burning olive branch and in ancient Greece athletes used olive oil to rub all over their bodies. The Bible contains more than one hundred forty references to olive oil, with the Koran and Hadith mentioning the value of olives numerous times.

The Egyptians and the Romans regarded the olive leaf as a symbol of power. Over time, it became a symbol of peace. This may have originated in Ancient Rome where the defeated would carry olive branches in order to seek peace. Olive trees are also believed to be associated with peace because it takes so long for a tree to mature and produce olives that it can only be cultivated in times of peace.

Besides food, in ancient times olive oil was used as a source of fuel for light and as a source of medicine for its healing powers. In about 400 B.C. the "Father of Medicine," Hippocrates, recommended olive oil as a cure for many different illnesses.

Today, olive oil is known by scientists worldwide for its antioxidants, Omega-3 fatty acids, monounsaturated fats, iron, vitamins A,B,C,D,E and K and phenols which reduce bad cholesterol, protect against heart disease, prevent cancer, and ease arthritis among many other things.

OLIVE OIL FALLS SOMEWHERE BETWEEN FOOD AND MEDICINE. Since ancient times, olives and olive oil have been used for food and to treat various diseases and maladies. Hippocrates was one of the first medical practitioners to record the health and therapeutic benefits of olive oil as a cure for mental illness, treatment for ulcers, healing of abrasions, for reducing muscular pain, and for soothing dry skin.

Modern science has validated these benefits and identified many more. Over the past few decades, many studies from researchers worldwide suggest that olive oil helps in the prevention of heart disease and cancer, promotes a healthy digestive system, reduces the effects of arthritis and offers protection against a host of other ailments.

HEART DISEASE

A diet that replaces most fat with olive oil has been proven to reduce the risk of cardiovascular disease. In recent years, several important studies have validated these results. The *Lyon Diet Heart Study* demonstrated the benefits of a Mediterranean style diet to dramatically lower cardiovascular disease risk.[1]

Olive oil with high phenolic content, particularly extra virgin olive oil, has anti-inflammatory and anti-clotting properties which result in healthier blood vessels and reduced cardiovascular disease.[2]

In November of 2004 the U.S. Food and Drug Administration (FDA) released the following statement:

> *Limited and not conclusive scientific evidence suggests that eating about 2 tablespoons (23 grams) of olive oil daily may reduce the risk of coronary heart disease due to the monounsaturated fat in olive oil.[3]*

17

HIGH BLOOD PRESSURE

According to Professor Dimitrios Trichopoulos, author and consulting epidemiologist at the University of Athens, "olive oil intake is inversely associated with both systolic and diastolic blood pressure"[4]

A new study in the Journal of Nutrition states that "moderate intake of olive oil was successful in reducing the blood pressure of healthy men who don't usually eat a Med-type diet."[5]

In a study published in March 2000, Italian researchers concluded that by reducing fat intake combined with using extra virgin olive oil, patients were able to lower their antihypertensive medication.[6]

CHOLESTEROL

The two main forms of cholesterol are high density lipoproteins (HDL) and low density lipoproteins (LDL). Essentially the HDL is good, and LDL is bad. Olive oil has been proven to lower LDL and raise HDL, resulting in reduced chances of coronary heart disease.[7]

BREAST CANCER

Oleic acid in olive oil has been proven to protect women against certain types of breast cancer. In a study conducted at Northwestern University by Dr. Javier Menendez, "we were able to demonstrate that the main component of olive oil, oleic acid, is able to down-regulate the most important oncogene in breast cancer. The most important source of oleic acid is olive oil."[8]

CANCER

In a recent study conducted in Europe, phenols in olive oil have been demonstrated to reduce leukemia cells.[9] There are also numerous studies identifying the protective benefits of olive oil on skin cancer, colon cancer, prostate cancer and other forms of cancer.

By examining the by-products of oxidation damage to cells, a precursor to cancer, in only three weeks researchers were able to significantly reduce the incidence of these compounds in patients who drank 25 ml of olive oil daily.

> "Determining the health benefits of any particular food is challenging because it involves relatively large numbers of people over significant periods of time," said lead investigator Henrik E. Poulsen, M.D. "In our study, we overcame these challenges by measuring how olive oil affected the oxidation of our genes, which is closely linked to development of disease. This approach allows us to determine if olive oil or any other food makes a difference. Our findings must be confirmed, but every piece of evidence so far points to olive oil being a healthy food. By the way, it also tastes great."[10]

ARTHRITIS

Studies have proven that a Mediterranean diet with most fat coming from olive oil results in a "reduction of inflammatory activity, an increase in physical function, and improved vitality" for patients with Rheumatoid Arthritis.[11]

CONCLUSION

THE HEALTH BENEFITS OF OLIVE OIL have been proven repeatedly by scientists around the world. Conducting a search for olive oil health benefits will return hundreds of scholarly research articles on the subject. Only a very small sampling is included here. The irrefutable fact is simply that olive oil consumption makes you healthier and prevents disease. The purpose of this cookbook is to help people to integrate healthy olive oil into their cooking and baking, providing delicious and healthy desserts for their family and friends.

(SEE ENDNOTES PAGE ??)

CLASSIFICATIONS & DEFINITIONS of OLIVE OILS

VIRGIN OLIVE OILS

EXTRA VIRGIN OLIVE OIL is obtained from the fruit of the olive tree by mechanical or other physical means that do not lead to deterioration of the oil. It does not undergo any treatment other than washing, decantation, centrifugation, and filtration.

FOUR GRADES OF OLIVE OIL ARE AVAILABLE TO RETAIL CONSUMERS

Extra Virgin Olive Oil: This is the fruity oil obtained from healthy, fresh green or ripe olives. How fruity it is depends on the variety and ripeness of the olives. This fruitiness can be perceived through both flavor and aroma. Extra virgin olive oil has no smell or taste defects.

Virgin Olive Oil: This oil has only the slightest taste and smell defects. When measured by professional tasters, the intensity of the defects must not be over a specified level. It must be perceptibly fruity.

Pure Olive Oil: This is the name given to the blend of refined olive oil and virgin olive oil. The proportion of each depends on consumer tastes. Virgin olive oil is added to the refined oil to restore flavor, aroma, color and antioxidants that are lost during refining.

Olive-Pomace Oil: This is the name given to the oil obtained by using solvents to extract the residual oil from the olive mash (olive pomace) that is left after producing virgin olive oil. It is then refined and blended with varying proportions of virgin olive oil. Blending gives the oil the flavor, odor, color, and antioxidants of virgin olive oil.

These four grades of olive oil and olive-pomace oil have the same nutritional value in that their fatty acid composition has a particularly high content of monounsaturated fatty acids. All four grades contain antioxidants, particularly

phenols and tocopherols, with extra virgin olive oil having the highest content. The organoleptic quality of the oils varies according to grade. Extra virgin olive oil, the most expensive oil, stands out because of its typical olive fruitiness and its high content of antioxidants.

The four grades are suitable for all kinds of cooking: frying, sautéing, roasting, sauces, salads, and baking. Choosing the right olive oil depends on personal taste. When buying olive oil, look beyond the advertising and read the label carefully to check the grade of oil inside.

Store all four grades in airtight containers away from light and at room temperature. Some sedimentation occurs at temperatures lower than 37 degrees Fahrenheit as certain constituents harden, but this disappears when the oil returns to room temperature.

It is important to check the "best before" or "bottled on" date on the label since the organoleptic quality of oil decreases with time.

PURE OLIVE OIL IS ALWAYS BEST FOR SWEET DESSERTS.

Always coat or spray all baking pans with olive oil to prevent sticking. This includes cookie sheets.

Keep olive oil away from light and heat. If you are not using your olive oil on a regular basis, it is best to store it in the refrigerator or freezer to prevent the oil from becoming rancid. When you're ready to bake, bring it back to room temperature and bake away!

If you plan on baking often, purchase your olive oil in bulk (in large containers). This may reduce your costs significantly. A great place to look for good prices on olive oil is at grocery warehouse stores.

When baking non-sweet breads and other foods, don't be afraid to use extra virgin or virgin olive oil. It tastes fantastic, and remember – it is very good for you.

ADD A LITTLE MORE NUTRITION into your desserts by substituting Whole Wheat Pastry Flour for white flour.

Whole Wheat Pastry Flour, a favorite for pastries, cookies, waffles, pancakes and biscuits, has a lower gluten and protein content and therefore is not generally used in making the typical loaf of bread (in fact, it won't work).

Whole Wheat Pastry Flour is ground from a soft pastry wheat berry. A different berry than your typical Red or White wheat berries, it has the same amount of fiber but is a bit lower in protein. Either way, when you use it to make your favorite desserts in substitution of white flour you will barely notice the difference. You can start slow by using half white and half Whole Wheat Pastry Flour or you can be very courageous and use only the pastry flour. Give it a try, you'll be pleasantly surprised!

Whole Wheat Pastry Flour can be found in the bulk aisle or on the shelf of your local health food store. Due to growing popularity, Whole Wheat Pastry Flour has become more mainstream and can usually be found at your neighborhood grocery store.

Recipes in this cookbook that are easily adapted to Whole Wheat Pastry Flour are marked with a wheat symbol.

WHEAT SYMBOL

WHOLE WHEAT PASTRY FLOUR NUTRITION FACTS:

SERVING SIZE: ¼ CUP (28 G)

NUTRIENT AMOUNT % DV

Calories 90
Calories from Fat 0
Total Fat 0 g 0%
Sodium 0 mg 0%

Total Carbohydrate 21 g 7%
Dietary Fiber 3 g 11%
Protein 4 g
Iron 6%

The Marathon Runner

Monte's dad had his first heart attack at age 52. He grew up on fried everything and lots of red meat. After bypass surgery and a few more years, his arteries were heavily clogged again, and his doctor told him to get his affairs in order and to begin saying his goodbyes. He has since gone on an extremely restrictive diet called the Ornish Diet. Now, at age 68, he has reversed his blockage and is doing well.

Regarding Monte, a 43-year-old runner, his heart and arteries look clear but his cholesterol hovered around 300 and he was at risk of developing problems. After watching what his father had been through, he said goodbye to red meat, dairy fats, real eggs and shrimp, and began to incorporate more insoluble fiber, fish and healthy oils, including olive oil, into his diet. Although he has the discipline, like his dad, to never eat anything good again, he's excited to have desserts that he can enjoy every now and again, and that won't make him feel like he's shortening his life with every bite.

—*Bobbi*

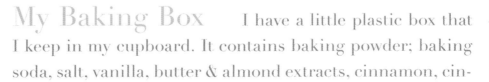

My Baking Box

I have a little plastic box that I keep in my cupboard. It contains baking powder; baking soda, salt, vanilla, butter & almond extracts, cinnamon, cinnamon sugar, yeast, chocolate chips, cooking spray and measuring spoons.

When it's time to bake, no need to go searching for all the small ingredients, I have everything I need in one little box.

Cakes

Chapter 1

About Dustings, Glazes, Sugars, & Toppings

You will notice in most all of my dessert recipes there is a lack of frosting. This is because these desserts are so rich and flavorful that there is rarely a need to add a thick and heavy frosting.

Dustings, glazes, sugars, and crumb-like toppings are lighter and add just the right amount of extra sweetness that I am sure you will enjoy.

So glaze, dust, sugar, and top away, and know that you are not giving up anything but extra fat and calories!!!

Happy Baking,
—*Micki*

Applesauce Cake  SERVES 12 to 16

What a great thing it is to use applesauce in a cake recipe. It allows you to cut back a little on sugar and fat. With a hint of four spices in every soft and filling bite, this applesauce cake does that and more.

INGREDIENTS

½ cup.................. pure olive oil
1 cup.................. brown sugar, packed
1 large .... egg
2 large .... egg whites
1½ cups .... applesauce
1 teaspoon........... cinnamon
1 teaspoon........... ginger
½ teaspoon.......... nutmeg
½ teaspoon.......... cloves
2 cups .... flour
2 teaspoons .... baking soda
1 teaspoon........... salt
1 cup.................. pecans, finely chopped
.... (optional)

GLAZE
1½ cups .... powdered sugar
1 teaspoon........... pure vanilla extract
5 tablespoons...... apple juice

PREPARATION

1. Preheat oven to 350°F. Coat one 9x13-inch baking pan or one bundt pan with olive oil cooking spray.

2. Cream together olive oil, brown sugar, egg, and egg whites.

3. Add applesauce, cinnamon, ginger, nutmeg, and cloves. Blend well.

4. Add flour, baking soda, and salt. Blend until well mixed. Fold in pecans.

5. Pour into prepared baking pan. Bake for 40 minutes or until a knife inserted into the center comes out clean.

GLAZE
In small mixing bowl add powdered sugar, vanilla, and apple juice. Mix until completely blended. Glaze cake while hot and let cool.

Basic Cream Cheese Frosting

Using light cream cheese cuts fat calories without compromising taste. It's the perfect frosting for Carrot Cake, or Dad's Cinnamon Rolls (page 64).

INGREDIENTS

8 ounces .... light cream cheese
4 cups .... powdered sugar
1½ teaspoons ...... pure vanilla extract
½ teaspoon.......... butter extract
½ teaspoon.......... salt

PREPARATION

In mixer bowl add cream cheese and beat on medium/high speed until smooth.
Add powdered sugar, vanilla & butter extracts, and salt. Blend until smooth and creamy.

BUTTER EXTRACT: *To add butter flavor to some of the recipes in this book, I have listed in the ingredients, "butter extract." This extract is a butter flavoring that does not contain butter at all. It can usually be found at you local grocery store in the spice section. If you can't find it there you are sure to find it online.*

Carrot Cake SERVES 12 to 16

My friend Judy makes this cake. It is packed with tasty ingredients. I made only a few changes and it tastes as wonderful as it always has! What's up Doc?

INGREDIENTS

½ cup................... pure olive oil
¼ cup................... pure maple syrup
2 cups .... brown sugar, packed
1 tablespoon .... honey
1 large .... egg
3 large .... egg whites
2½ cups .... flour
2 teaspoons .... baking powder
1 teaspoon........... baking soda
1 teaspoon........... salt
2 teaspoons .... cinnamon
½ teaspoon........... nutmeg
½ teaspoon........... cloves
2½ cups .... grated carrots
2 teaspoons .... fresh lemon juice
2 teaspoons .... pure vanilla extract
1 small can .... crushed pineapple,
            about ½ cup, juice included
1 cup.................... pecans, finely chopped
            (optional)

PREPARATION

1. Preheat oven to 350°F. Coat one 9x13-inch baking pan with olive oil cooking spray.

2. In mixer bowl add olive oil, maple syrup, brown sugar, honey, egg, and egg whites. Mix until smooth and creamy.

3. Add flour, baking powder, baking soda, salt, cinnamon, nutmeg, and cloves. Blend until well mixed.

4. Add carrots, lemon juice, vanilla, pineapple, and chopped nuts. Blend again.

5. Pour into prepared pan. Bake for 55~60 minutes or until a knife inserted into the center comes out clean. Cool completely.

6. Dust with powdered sugar or frost with basic cream cheese frosting. (see page 32)

Chocolate Chip Buttermilk Cake SERVES 12 to 16

My son Chris says, "This cake tastes like a chocolate chip cookie only it's a cake!"

INGREDIENTS

¾ cup.................... pure olive oil
1¾ cups .... granulated sugar
1 cup.................... buttermilk
2 teaspoons .... pure vanilla extract
4 large .... eggs
2 cups .... all purpose flour
½ teaspoon.......... baking powder
1 teaspoon........... baking soda
½ teaspoon.......... salt
1 cup.................... mini chocolate chips

COCOA DUSTING

1 cup.................... powdered sugar
1 tablespoon .... cocoa powder
                (Dutch milled is best)

PREPARATION

1. Preheat oven to 350°F. Coat one 9x13-inch pan with olive oil cooking spray.

2. In mixer bowl add olive oil, sugar, buttermilk, vanilla, and eggs. Blend on medium speed for 1~2 minutes.

3. Add flour, baking powder, baking soda, and salt. Mix until well blended.

4. Gently fold in chocolate chips.

5. Pour into prepared pan. Bake 40~45 minutes or until a knife inserted into the center comes out clean. Remove and cool completely.

COCOA DUST PREPARATION

In small mixing bowl add powdered sugar and cocoa powder. Mix until completely blended. Use a shaker or a fine strainer to dust the top of the cooled cake.

There are four basic food groups:
milk chocolate, dark chocolate,
white chocolate,
and chocolate truffles.
—Author Unknown

Chocolate Lava Lava Cake SERVES 8

A flourless cake that is truly to die for. Like a volcano, crispy on the outside, soft on the inside. Best if served right away. You could store it in the refrigerator... but you won't want to!

INGREDIENTS

¼ cup.................. pure olive oil
¾ cup.................. semi-sweet chocolate chips
4 large .... eggs, separated, discard 1 yolk
1 tablespoon .... granulated sugar
⅓ cup .... granulated sugar
½ teaspoon.......... butter extract
2 teaspoons .... pure vanilla extract

COCOA DUST
½ cup .... powdered sugar
1½ teaspoons ...... dark cocoa powder
(Dutch milled is best)

PREPARATION

1. Preheat oven to 400°F. Generously spray 8 individual ramekin dishes with olive oil cooking spray. Place on a cookie sheet (for balance and over-spills).

2. In a microwavable bowl add olive oil and chocolate. Melt on high for about 1 minute. Stir until completely melted and set aside.

3. In mixer bowl add egg whites and beat on high speed until soft peaks form. Turn mixer to low speed and slowly add 1 tablespoon of sugar and beat for another minute.

4. In mixing bowl add 3 egg yolks, 1/3 cup sugar, butter and vanilla extracts. Beat until smooth and creamy.

5. Fold chocolate mixture into egg yolk mixture.

6. Using a spatula or large spoon, fold egg white mixture into chocolate mixture until completely blended.

7. Pour approximately ¾ cup into prepared ramekin dishes. Bake for 11~14 minutes. Outside should be crusted. Remove and let sit for 5 minutes.

COCOA DUST PREPARATION
In small mixing bowl add powdered sugar and cocoa powder. Mix until completely blended. Use a shaker or a fine mesh strainer to dust the top of the cooled cake. Garnish with a couple sprigs of mint.

SUGGESTION: *Add a small scoop of vanilla bean ice cream or frozen yogurt on the side, and you are in heaven.*

Comfort Cake SERVES 12 to 16

The name says it all. Eat a piece, and then eat another. Then share it with someone before you eat the whole cake.

INGREDIENTS

1 box.................... devils food cake mix
1 small box .... instant chocolate pudding mix
1 cup.................... low fat vanilla yogurt
½ cup.................... pure olive oil
4 large .... eggs
¾ cup.................... warm water 110°F ~ 115°F
                              (baby bottle warm)
1 large package .... mini semi-sweet chocolate chips
½ cup.................... powdered sugar

PREPARATION

1. Preheat oven to 350°F. Coat one 9x13-inch pan or 12-18 muffin tins with olive oil cooking spray.

2. In mixer bowl add cake mix, pudding mix, yogurt, eggs, and olive oil. Blend on medium speed for 1~2 minutes.

3. Turn mixer onto low speed and slowly add water. Mix until well blended. Fold in chocolate chips.

4. Pour into prepared pan. Bake for 45 minutes or until a knife inserted into the center comes out clean. Cool in pan for 30 minutes.

5. Using a shaker or fine strainer, dust with powdered sugar.

Dave's Infamous German Chocolate Cake

Serves 12 to 16

It wouldn't be fair if I didn't include my sweetheart's incredible German Chocolate Cake recipe in this book. Yes, I have changed it and made it with olive oil!

INGREDIENTS

1/8-ounce	"German" sweet chocolate squares
½ cup	boiling water
4 large	egg whites
⅔ cup	pure olive oil
2 cups	granulated sugar
4 large	egg yolks, unbeaten
1 teaspoons	pure vanilla extract
1 cup	vanilla yogurt
2¼ cups	all purpose flour
1 teaspoon	baking soda
½ teaspoon	salt

COCONUT PECAN FROSTING

1 cup	evaporated milk
1 cup	granulated sugar
3 large	egg yolks
⅓ cup	pure olive oil
1 teaspoon	pure vanilla extract
1 teaspoon	butter extract
1 cup	shredded coconut
1 cup	finely chopped pecans

PREPARATION

1. Preheat oven to 350°F. Coat one 9x13-inch pan with olive oil cooking spray.

2. Place chocolate squares in ½ cup boiling water. Stir until melted. Set aside.

3. In mixer bowl, beat egg whites until stiff but not dry. Pour into another bowl and set aside.

4. In separate mixer bowl add olive oil, sugar, and egg yolks. Mix until well blended.

5. Add chocolate-water mixture, vanilla, and yogurt. Blend until well mixed.

6. Add flour, baking soda, and salt. Blend again.

7. Fold in stiff egg whites and stir until just mixed.

8. Pour into prepared pans. Bake 40~50 minutes or until a knife inserted into the center comes out clean. Remove and cool completely in pan.

FROSTING PREPARATION

1. In a saucepan, combine evaporated milk, sugar, egg yolks, and olive oil. Stir over medium heat until mixture thickens (about 12 minutes).

2. Remove from heat, add vanilla & butter extracts, coconut, and pecans. Mix by hand until blended.

3. Cool for about 10 minutes. Spread on top of cooled cake.

Bake for someone's birthday. You never know, it just might be his or her favorite cake!

For the first 12 years of our marriage

my husband would give me a surprise party for my birthday every year. I always knew that some kind of surprise was coming, but it was something different every year. He would also make me a German Chocolate Cake from scratch every year. He spent hours doing it and was so proud of how well he made the cake. He assumed that I loved it and that it was my favorite. Well, the years got busy and he didn't make the cake for a long time. Then a few years ago, he proudly made it again. I always went along, but the truth is, I never have, do not now, and never will like German Chocolate Cake. But I do love the man that makes it.

Sorry Honey.

—*Micki*

Ginger Apple Cake SERVES 12 to 16

This is a favorite of mine to make in the fall, when the apples are at their best. The only way to improve upon this cake is to share it with a dear friend.

INGREDIENTS

1 large .... apple, peeled and chopped
(Fujis are best)
2 tablespoons ...... brown sugar, packed
1 tablespoon .... fresh lemon juice
⅔ cup .... pure olive oil
⅔ cup .... granulated sugar
1 large .... egg, beaten
2 large .... egg whites, beaten
½ cup.................. molasses
1 teaspoon........... cinnamon
½ teaspoon.......... nutmeg
½ teaspoon.......... cloves
½ teaspoon.......... ginger
2½ cups .... flour
½ teaspoon.......... baking powder
1½ teaspoons ...... baking soda
1 teaspoon........... salt
1 cup................... boiling water

GLAZE
2 cups .... powdered suger
¼ cups .... milk
1 tablespoon .... lemon juice
1 pinch .... salt

PREPARATION

1. Preheat oven to 375°F. Coat one 9x13-inch pan with olive oil cooking spray.

2. In a small mixing bowl, blend chopped apples with brown sugar and lemon juice. Set aside.

3. In mixer bowl add olive oil, sugar, egg, and egg whites. Blend until smooth.

4. Add molasses, cinnamon, nutmeg, cloves and ginger. Mix until well blended.

5. Add flour, baking powder, baking soda, and salt. Blend again.

6. On low speed, slowly add boiling water and mix until smooth and creamy (scraping sides if necessary).

7. Gently fold in apple/sugar mixture.

8. Pour into prepared pan. Bake for 35~40 minutes or until a knife inserted into the center comes out clean. Remove and glaze immediately.

GLAZE PREPARATION
In small mixing bowl, add powdered sugar, milk, vanilla, and salt. Mix until well blended. Spread evenly over cake while hot.

Never eat more than you can lift.

Miss Piggy

Good 'Ole Texas
Sheet Cake SERVES 24 to 28

This thin moist cake, that is the size of Texas, is sure to be a crowd pleaser and will keep y'all comin' back for more!!!

INGREDIENTS

2 cups	all purpose flour
2 cups	granulated sugar
1 teaspoon	baking soda
½ teaspoon	salt
¾ cup	pure olive oil
¼ cup	cocoa powder (Dutch milled is best)
2 large	eggs, beaten
½ cup	low-fat buttermilk
1 teaspoon	pure vanilla extract
1 teaspoon	butter extract
1 cup	hot water

FROSTING

¼ cup	pure olive oil
½ cup	buttermilk
4 tablespoons	cocoa powder
1 teaspoon	pure vanilla extract
1 pound	powdered sugar (4 cups)
1 cup	pecans or coconut, finely chopped (optional)

PREPARATION

1. Preheat oven to 400°F. Coat one 18x12-inch jelly roll pan with olive oil cooking spray and set aside.

2. In mixer bowl combine flour, sugar, baking soda, and salt. Set aside.

3. In a saucepan, over medium heat, combine; olive oil, cocoa, and water. While continually stirring, slowly bring to a boil. Stir for 1 minute more and remove from heat.

4. Add chocolate mixture to flour mixture and blend on medium speed for 1~1½ minutes.

5. Add eggs, buttermilk, and vanilla & butter extracts, mix until smooth. Slowly add hot water and mix until completely blended (batter will be watery).

6. Pour onto prepared jelly roll pan and bake for 20 minutes or until top springs back when touched. Remove and frost immediately.

FROSTING PREPARATION

1. In a saucepan, over medium heat, combine olive oil, buttermilk, and cocoa. While stirring, bring to a low boil.

2. Remove from heat, add vanilla and powdered sugar. Mix until smooth. Spread evenly over hot cake.

3. Sprinkle with chopped pecans or coconut.

Honey Cakes SERVES 9 to 12

Honey cakes are a traditional middle-east confection. A very simple, whole-wheat, sugar & egg free treat for even the pickiest of dessert lovers.

INGREDIENTS

½ cup .... toasted sesame seeds
1½ cups .... whole wheat pastry flour
½ teaspoon .... salt
½ cup.................. pure olive oil
⅔ cup.................. honey

PREPARATION

1. Preheat oven to 350°F. Coat one 8X8-inch baking pan with olive oil cooking spray.

2. In a medium size mixing bowl, add all ingredients and mix until well blended.

3. Spread evenly into prepared pan and bake for 25-30 minutes or until a knife inserted into the center comes out clean. Serve hot or cold.

Pineapple Coconut Cake  SERVES 8 to 10

I first baked this cake and served it at a tasting party I was hosting in my home. It was the hit of the evening. I hope you enjoy this tasty cake as much as everyone did that night.

INGREDIENTS

²/₃ cup .... pure olive oil
2 teaspoons .... lemon zest
1 cup.................... granulated sugar
2 large .... eggs
1 large .... egg white
1 teaspoon.......... pure vanilla extract
¾ cup.................. pineapple juice
½ cup.................. shredded coconut
2 cups .... flour
2 teaspoons .... baking powder
1 teaspoon.......... salt

PINEAPPLE GLAZE
2 cups .... powdered sugar
1 teaspoon.......... pure vanilla extract
⅓ cup .... pineapple juice

PREPARATION

1. Preheat oven to 350°F. Coat one 9x9-inch pan with olive oil cooking spray.

2. In mixer bowl add olive oil, lemon zest, sugar, eggs, and egg white. Blend on medium speed for 1 minute.

3. Add vanilla, pineapple juice, and coconut, and mix until well blended.

4. Add flour, baking powder, and salt. Blend until smooth.

5. Pour into prepared pan. Bake for 35~40 minutes or until top turns brown and a knife inserted into the center comes out clean. Glaze cake while warm and cool completely.

GLAZE PREPARATION
In mixing bowl combine olive oil, powdered sugar, vanilla, and pineapple juice. Blend until smooth.

Silky Cheesecake with Strawberries SERVES 8 to 10

Silky really describes this soft, airy, lower fat, New York Style Cheesecake. The best time to bake this is when the strawberries are in season and plentiful, or when you want a little taste of the Big Apple.

INGREDIENTS

1 recipe .... Graham Cracker Crust (see page 122)
3 large .... egg whites
¼ cup.................. granulated sugar
12 ounces .... Light or Neufchatel cream cheese, softened
1 cup.................. granulated sugar
2 large .... egg yolks
1½ tablespoons ... pure vanilla extract
1¾ cups .... low fat vanilla yogurt
¼ cup.................. flour
¼ teaspoon.......... salt

TOPPING
2 cups .... fresh or frozen strawberries chopped
½ cup.................. strawberry jam
1 teaspoon........... pure vanilla extract

PREPARATION

1. Preheat oven to 300°F. Prepare Graham Cracker Crust in springform pan (cheesecake pan).

2. In mixer bowl, add egg whites and beat on high speed until soft peaks form. Turn mixer on low speed and gradually add sugar. Increase speed to medium/high and beat for another minute. Pour mixture into a separate mixing bowl and set aside.

3. In mixer bowl add cream cheese, sugar, egg yolks, vanilla, and yogurt. Blend until smooth and creamy.

4. Add flour and salt. Blend again until well mixed.

5. Using a spatula, gently fold egg white mixture into batter and lightly blend in.

6. Pour into prepared crust. Bake 50~60 minutes. Turn off oven, leaving door closed, remove and allow cake to sit for an additional 30 minutes.

7. Remove and cool completely in pan. Place in the refrigerator to chill for a minimum of 2 hours.

TOPPING PREPARATION
In a small bowl, blend strawberries, jam and vanilla. Serve topping on the side.

Sweet & Slow
Banana Cake SERVES 12 to 16

A moist banana cake takes some time to prepare. This is one of those things in life that fits the phrase, "If it is well worth it, it is worth waiting for."

INGREDIENTS

1½ cups .... over-ripe bananas, mashed (about 4 small or 2 ½ large bananas)
2 teaspoons .... lemon juice
1 tablespoon ...... lemon zest
⅔ cup .... pure olive oil
1 cup .... granulated sugar
1 cup .... brown sugar
3 large .... eggs
2 teaspoons .... pure vanilla extract
1 teaspoon .... butter extract
3 cups .... all purpose flour
1½ teaspoons ..... baking soda
½ teaspoon .... salt
1½ cups .... buttermilk
1 cup .... chopped pecans (optional)

PREPARATION

1. Preheat oven to 275°F. Coat a 9x13-inch pan with olive oil cooking spray.

2. In a small mixing bowl, blend together bananas, lemon juice, and lemon zest. Set aside.

3. In a mixer bowl place olive oil, sugar, and brown sugar. Mix on medium speed for one minute.

4. Add eggs and vanilla & butter extracts. Mix for another minute.

5. Add flour, baking soda and salt. Blend well.

6. With mixer on low speed, add buttermilk and blend until well mixed.

7. Add banana mixture and blend again for another minute.

8. Pour into prepared pan. Bake for 1 hour and 15 minutes or until a knife inserted into the center comes out clean.

9. Remove, place in the freezer for 1~2 hours. Frost with basic cream cheese frosting (see page 32). Top with chopped pecans.

Yogurt Coffee Cake SERVES 8 to 10

The yogurt in this coffee cake adds an additional softness and light sweetness that everyone is sure to savor.

INGREDIENTS

⅓ cup .... pure olive oil
1 cup.................... granulated sugar
2 large .... eggs
1 cup.................... low fat vanilla yogurt
1 teaspoon........... pure vanilla extract
1 teaspoon........... butter extract
2 cups .... flour
1 teaspoon........... baking powder
1 teaspoon........... baking soda
½ teaspoon.......... salt

CRUMB TOPPING

¼ cup................... flour
¾ cup................... brown sugar, packed
1 cup.................... walnuts, finely chopped
¼ cup................... pure olive oil
¼ teaspoon.......... salt

PREPARATION

1. Preheat oven to 350°F. Coat a 9x9-inch square baking pan with olive oil cooking spray.

2. In mixer bowl add olive oil, sugar, eggs, yogurt, and vanilla & butter extracts. Blend on medium speed until smooth and creamy.

3. Add flour, baking powder, baking soda, and salt. Mix until smooth.

4. Pour ½ of the batter into the pan. Sprinkle ½ of the crumb mixture evenly over top. Pour the other half of the batter and cover middle crumb topping. Sprinkle on remaining crumb topping.

5. Bake 45~50 minutes or until a knife inserted into the center comes out clean. Cool and serve.

CRUMB TOPPING PREPARATION

In mixing bowl add flour, brown sugar, walnuts, olive oil, and salt. Cut together with a fork. Topping will be crumbly.

Cookies &Bars

Chapter 2

A New Toll Cookie

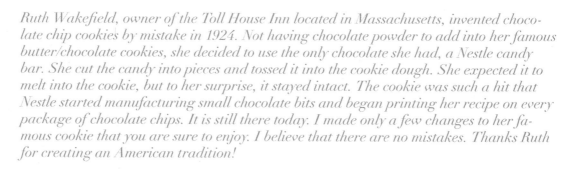

Ruth Wakefield, owner of the Toll House Inn located in Massachusetts, invented choco-late chip cookies by mistake in 1924. Not having chocolate powder to add into her famous butter/chocolate cookies, she decided to use the only chocolate she had, a Nestle candy bar. She cut the candy into pieces and tossed it into the cookie dough. She expected it to melt into the cookie, but to her surprise, it stayed intact. The cookie was such a hit that Nestle started manufacturing small chocolate bits and began printing her recipe on every package of chocolate chips. It is still there today. I made only a few changes to her fa-mous cookie that you are sure to enjoy. I believe that there are no mistakes. Thanks Ruth for creating an American tradition!

INGREDIENTS

⅔ cup	pure olive oil
¾ cup	granulated sugar
¾ cup	brown sugar, packed
2 large	eggs
2 teaspoons	pure vanilla extract
1 teaspoon	butter extract
1 tablespoon	milk
2½ cups	flour
1 teaspoon	baking soda
1 teaspoon	salt
1 cup	semi-sweet chocolate chips
1 cup	chopped pecans (optional)

PREPARATION

1. Preheat oven to 375°F. Lightly coat large cookie sheets with olive oil cooking spray.

2. In a mixer bowl add olive oil, sugar, and brown sugar. Blend until smooth and creamy. Beat in eggs, vanilla & butter extracts, and milk.

3. Add flour, baking soda, and salt. Blend well.

4. Fold in chocolate chips and pecans. Drop by tablespoonfuls or medium size cookie scoop onto prepared cookie sheets.

5. Bake 9~11 minutes. Cool on wire racks.

Sacrificing for Chocolate Chip Cookies

Ashleigh was making chocolate chip cookies once, while we were dating. Everything was going well until she attempted to clean the excess dough from the mixing attachment. As she reached in to knock the cookie dough loose, she bumped the "on" switch to the Kitchenaid and the trouble had officially begun. Before she could react to the mixer being on, her hand was caught, tangled in the attachment. Luckily it did not hurt her, but made her laugh at the situation she found herself in. (For those of you who might be wondering, the cookies turned out OK.)

—Randy

Black Bottom
Toffee Chip Cookies  SERVES 36 TO 42

I made these by accident and everybody loved them. Talk about comfort food. WOW!

INGREDIENTS

½ cup	semi-sweet or milk chocolate chips
¾ cup	pure olive oil
1½ cups	brown sugar, packed
1 large	egg, beaten
1 large	egg white, beaten
2 teaspoons	pure vanilla extract
2¼ cups	flour
1 teaspoon	baking soda
½ teaspoon	salt
1 cup	toffee chips
½ cup	semi-sweet or milk chocolate chips

PREPARATION

1. Preheat oven to 375°F. Lightly coat large cookie sheets with olive oil cooking spray.

2. In small glass bowl, melt chocolate chips in microwave for 45-60 seconds and set aside.

3. In mixer bowl add olive oil, brown sugar, egg, egg whites, and vanilla. Blend until smooth.

4. Add flour, baking soda, and salt, and blend well. Fold in toffee chips.

5. Bake 9~11 minutes or until light brown. Cool on wire racks for 10 minutes.

6. Spread bottom side of cookies with melted chocolate and place upside down on a plate or cookie sheets. Put in freezer for 15 minutes or until chocolate is firm to the touch. Bring back to room temperature and enjoy!

Research tells us fourteen out of any ten individuals like chocolate.
—Sandra Boynton

Candy Bar Cookies SERVES 36 TO 42

I love to make this cookie sometime after Halloween. I have been known to "borrow" candy bars from my children's stash. I figure they won't miss the candy if I share my cookies with them. No complaints so far.

INGREDIENTS

⅔ cup .... pure olive oil
2 cups .... brown sugar, packed
2 large .... eggs
½ cup .... milk
2 teaspoons .... pure vanilla extract
½ teaspoon .... butter extract
2½ cups .... flour
1 teaspoon .... baking powder
½ teaspoon .... baking soda
½ teaspoon .... salt
3½ cups .... quick oats
1, 8-ounce .... chocolate candy bar (pick your favorite & chop it up)

PREPARATION

1. Preheat oven to 375°F. Lightly coat large cookie sheets with olive oil cooking spray.

2. In large mixing bowl, blend olive oil, brown sugar, eggs, milk, and vanilla & butter extracts. Mix until smooth and creamy.

3. Add flour, baking powder, baking soda, salt, and oats. Blend until well mixed.

4. Fold in chopped candy bar. Drop by heaping teaspoonfuls or small size cookie scoop.

5. Bake 8~10 minutes. Cool and enjoy!

CHOCOLATE TIDBIT: *Did you know that by melting a cup of chocolate and 2-3 tablespoons of olive oil, you will have a perfect ice cream topper that hardens as it hits the frozen ice cream? Store unused in a sealed container on the shelf.*

Chocolate Sin Cookie SERVES 36 TO 42

Some days are just chocolate days. Other days are DARK Chocolate days. On those days, this cookie is for you!

INGREDIENTS

½ cup .... pure olive oil
1½ cups .... granulated sugar
3 large .... eggs, beaten
3 Tablespoons ..... milk
2 teaspoons .... pure vanilla extract
½ cup .... unsweetened cocoa
                       (Dutch milled is best)
2⅔ cups .... flour
2 teaspoons .... baking powder
¾ teaspoon .... salt
¾ cups .... granulated sugar
24 .... chocolate chunks
                       (use your favorite)

PREPARATION

1. Preheat oven to 375°F. Lightly coat large cookie sheets with olive oil cooking spray.

2. In mixer bowl add olive oil, sugar, eggs, and milk. Mix until well blended.

3. Add vanilla and cocoa. Blend until smooth.

4. Add flour, baking powder, and salt. Mix until well blended.

5. Drop by teaspoonfuls or by small size cookie scoop into powdered sugar and roll until coated. Place 3 per row (these cookies spread).

6. Bake for 7~10 minutes. Remove from oven and press a chunk of chocolate into the center of each cookie. Cool on wire racks and dive in!!!

TIME SAVING TIDBIT: *To save time, when baking cookies, double the batch and bake half. Store the second batch in the freezer so that you have dough on hand to thaw and quickly bake for a housewarming, a friend who is feeling down, or for someone who just neeeeeeeds some "Chocolate Sin Cookies".*

Crispy Rice Treats SERVES 12 TO 16

A new twist on an old favorite and you still can't eat just one.

INGREDIENTS

¼ cup.................... pure olive oil
1 teaspoon........... butter extract
1 teaspoon........... pure vanilla extract
12 ounces............. mini marshmallows (4½ cups)
6 cups .... crispy rice cereal

PREPARATION

1. Coat one 9x13-inch baking pan with olive oil cooking spray.

2. In a large pot heat olive oil on medium. Add marshmallows and stir until melted.

3. Remove from heat. Add butter and vanilla extracts.

4. Fold in cereal and stir until completely coated.

5. Pour into prepared baking dish and press down evenly. Cool, cut and say good-bye to these yummy treats!

This recipe can be doubled.

Extreme Lemon Sugar Cookies

SERVES 32 TO 36

If you love lemon, you will love these cookies. We have a hard time waiting for these babies to cool before we start to eat them!

INGREDIENTS

⅔ cup .... pure olive oil
1 cup.................... granulated sugar
1 large .... egg
2½ teaspoons ...... pure vanilla extract
2 tablespoons...... lemon zest (one large lemon)
2 tablespoons...... fresh lemon juice
2¼ cups .... flour
1 teaspoon........... baking powder
½ teaspoon.......... baking soda
½ teaspoon.......... salt
½ cup.................. additional sugar for rolling
½ cup................. powdered sugar for dusting.

PREPARATION

1. Preheat oven to 375°F. Coat cookie sheets with olive oil cooking spray.

2. In mixer bowl add olive oil, sugar, egg, vanilla, lemon zest, and lemon juice. Blend until smooth.

3. Add flour, baking powder, baking soda, and salt. Mix until well blended.

4. Drop by teaspoonfuls or by small size cookie scoop into sugar and roll until well coated. Place on prepared cookie sheets.

5. Bake 8 minutes, cool on wire racks, dust with powdered sugar.

LEMON JUICING TIDBIT: *One medium lemon will give you about two tablespoons of lemon juice. To make things easy, microwave your lemon for ten seconds and always squeeze your lemons cut side up so the seeds stay with the lemon and don't fall into your food!*

Grandma J's Oatmeal Cookies

My dear friend Val has been making this recipe for years. I have adjusted it just enough to keep that old fashioned soft cookie taste, and made it healthier. Craisins give it an added zing!

INGREDIENTS

½ cup.................. pure olive oil
½ cup.................. brown sugar, packed
½ cup.................. granulated sugar
1 large .... egg
2 teaspoons .... pure vanilla extract
1 teaspoon.......... butter extract
1 cup.................. flour
½ teaspoon.......... baking soda
½ teaspoon.......... baking powder
¼ teaspoon.......... salt
1 cup.................. quick oats
1 cup.................. Craisins (or raisins)

PREPARATION

1. Preheat oven to 350°F. Lightly coat large cookie sheets with olive oil cooking spray.

2. In mixer bowl blend olive oil, sugars, egg, and vanilla & butter extracts. Beat on medium/high speed until well mixed.

3. Add flour, baking soda, baking powder, and salt. Mix until well blended.

4. Fold in oats and Craisins (or raisins).

5. Drop by tablespoonfuls or medium size cookie scoop onto prepared cookie sheets.

6. Bake for 8~10 minutes. Cool on wire racks.

Lemon Laced Oatmeal Blueberry Cookies

SERVES 32 TO 36

These oatmeal cookies are to die for because they are laced with lemon throughout!!!

INGREDIENTS

⅔ cup .... pure olive oil
⅓ cup .... granulated sugar
⅓ cup .... brown sugar, packed
1 large .... egg
1 large .... egg white
1½ tablespoons ... lemon zest
2 tablespoons ...... fresh lemon juice
1 teaspoon .... pure vanilla extract
1½ cups .... flour
1 cup.................. quick oats
1 teaspoon .... baking powder
½ teaspoon .... baking soda
½ teaspoon .... salt
½ cup.................. dried, raisin-like blueberries
1½ cups .... crispy rice cereal

GLAZE
1 cup.................. powdered sugar
2 tablespoons ...... fresh lemon juice
½ teaspoon .... pure vanilla extract

PREPARATION

1. Preheat oven to 350°F. Lightly coat large cookie sheets with olive oil cooking spray.

2. In mixer bowl add olive oil, sugar, brown sugar, egg, egg white, lemon juice, lemon zest, and vanilla. Blend on medium speed until smooth and creamy.

3. Add flour, oats, baking powder, baking soda, and salt. Mix until well blended.

4. Fold in crispy rice cereal and blueberries.

5. Drop by tablespoonfuls or medium size cookie scoop onto prepared cookie sheets.

6. Bake for 9~11 minutes or until slightly browned. Remove, place on wire racks and glaze while hot.

GLAZE PREPARATION
In a small plastic zip bag add powdered sugar, lemon juice, and vanilla. Remove air and tightly seal bag. Massage bag until glaze is well mixed. Cut a small hole in the corner of the bag and using a back and forth motion, drizzle over cookies.

BROWN SUGAR TIDBIT: *Have you ever had your brown sugar as hard as a rock? Try this: Place a slice of fresh bread in the package of sugar. Be sure that the bag is sealed. Leave it to rest overnight and your sugar will be soft again.*

Lemony Squares
with Blueberries SERVES 9 TO 12

My Lemony Squares have just the right amount of coconut baked right into the crust. They may be small, but they pack a powerful punch. Pucker up and enjoy!

INGREDIENTS

BOTTOM CRUST

1 cup....................	flour
⅓ cup	pure olive oil
½ cup...................	powdered sugar
½ cup...................	flaked coconut

FILLING

3 large	eggs
1 cup....................	granulated sugar
3 tablespoons......	fresh lemon juice
1 tablespoon	lemon zest (about 1 lemon)
2 tablespoons......	flour
½ teaspoon..........	baking powder
¼ tsp...................	salt
1 teaspoon...........	pure vanilla extract
½ cup	powdered sugar for dusting
½ cup...................	fresh or frozen blueberries for topping

PREPARATION

1. Preheat oven to 350°F. Coat an 8x8-inch baking dish with olive oil cooking spray.

2. In mixing bowl combine flour, olive oil, powdered sugar, and coconut. Press into the bottom of prepared pan.

FILLING PREPARATION

1. In a medium mixing bowl add eggs, sugar, lemon juice, lemon zest, flour, baking powder, salt, and vanilla. Blend (by hand) until well mixed.

2. Spoon over prepared crust.

3. Bake for 15~20 minutes or until top is light brown. Remove, cool completely and dust top with ½ cup powdered sugar.. Cut into squares and top with blueberries.

LEMON ZEST TIDBIT: *Lemon zest is obtained by finely grating the outermost peel of a lemon. One medium lemon yields about one tablespoon of zest. As an added bonus, the zest of the lemon contains all of the essential oils in the fruit. It freezes well, too!*

Macadamia Crunchers 32 TO 36 COOKIES

Crunchy on the outside, chewy on the inside. ALOHA!!

INGREDIENTS

⅔ cup .... pure olive oil
1½ cups .... powdered sugar
⅔ cup .... brown sugar, packed
3 tablespoons ...... milk
1 large .... egg
2 large .... egg whites
1½ teaspoons ...... pure vanilla extract
1 teaspoon .... butter extract
2 cups .... all purpose flour
½ teaspoon .... baking powder
1 teaspoon .... baking soda
½ teaspoon .... salt
¾ cup .... macadamia nuts, chopped
1 cup .... crispy rice cereal
1 cup .... vanilla baking chips

PREPARATION

1. Preheat oven to 375°F. Coat cookie sheets with olive oil cooking spray.

2. In mixer bowl add olive oil, powdered sugar, brown sugar, milk, egg, egg whites, and vanilla & butter extracts. Blend on high speed for 2 minutes.

3. Add flour, baking powder, baking soda, and salt. Blend well.

4. Fold in macadamia nuts, crispy rice cereal, and vanilla chips.

5. Drop by teaspoonfuls or small size cookie scoop onto prepared baking sheets.

6. Bake for 8-10 minutes or until cookies are light brown.

Micki's Simple Brownies

SERVES 9 TO 12 SQUARES

This is an old-fashioned brownie. Because of the air whipped into the first stage of this recipe, it comes out crunchy and chewy. To make these brownies even more decadent, add chocolate chips.

INGREDIENTS

4 ounces .... unsweetened chocolate
baking squares
⅓ cup .... pure olive oil
3 large .... eggs
1½ cups .... granulated sugar
2 teaspoons .... pure vanilla extract
¾ cup................... flour
½ teaspoon.......... salt

FOR ADDED DECADENCE
½ cup................... semi-sweet chocolate chips

PREPARATION

1. Preheat oven to 375°F. Coat an 8x8-inch pan with olive oil cooking spray.

2. Place chocolate and olive oil in a small glass mixing bowl. Heat in microwave for 1 minute. Stir until melted and smooth. Set aside.

3. In mixer bowl add eggs, sugar, and vanilla and mix on medium/high speed for 5 minutes.

4. Add in chocolate mixture and blend until smooth and creamy.

5. Fold in flour and salt. Mix until just moistened. Do not overmix. If adding chocolate chips, gently blend in.

6. Bake for 20~25 minutes or until a knife inserted into the center comes out clean. Remove, cool slightly. Serve and enjoy!

Oatmeal Pecan Chewies

A delightful mix of oats, pecans, and coconut that brings out the natural goodness a hearty cookie is meant to have.

INGREDIENTS

⅔ cup .... pure olive oil
½ cup.................. granulated sugar
1½ cups .... brown sugar, packed
2 large .... eggs
2 teaspoons .... pure vanilla extract
1¼ cups .... flour
1 teaspoon........... baking powder
½ teaspoon.......... baking soda
1 teaspoon........... salt
2 cups .... quick oats
½ cup.................. pecans, chopped
1 cup................... flaked coconut
½ cup.................. raisins (optional)

PREPARATION

1. Preheat oven to 375°F. Lightly coat large cookie sheets with olive oil cooking spray.

2. In mixer bowl add olive oil, sugar, and brown sugar. Blend until smooth and creamy.

3. Add eggs and vanilla and blend on high speed for one minute.

4. Add flour, baking powder, baking soda, and salt. Blend well.

5. Add oats, pecans, coconut, and raisins.

6. Drop by teaspoonfuls or small size cookie scoop onto prepared cookie sheets.

7. Bake for 10~12 minutes. Cool on wire racks.

Olive Oil Short Bread SERVES 12 TO 16

A traditional favorite during the holidays. Fast, Easy and Tasty!

INGREDIENTS

¾ cup.................... pure olive oil
½ cup.................... powdered sugar
¼ cup.................... brown sugar
1 teaspoon........... butter extract
1 teaspoon........... pure vanilla extract
1½ cup................. flour
1 teaspoon........... salt
½ cup.................... cornstarch
½ teaspoon.......... cinnamon
½ teaspoon.......... nutmeg
½ cup.................... granulated sugar

PREPARATION

1. Preheat oven to 350°F. Lightly coat 9x9-inch pan with olive oil cooking spray.

2. In mixer bowl, combine all ingredients and blend on medium to high speed until dough is smooth.

3. Press mixture into bottom of prepared pan. Slice into rectangular shapes and score with a fork before baking.

4. Bake for 35~40 minutes. Let cool for 45 minutes. When cool and while in pan, slice again and roll in sugar.

Top 10 Reasons to Eat Oatmeal

10. Oatmeal may lower cholesterol and reduce the risk of heart disease.

9. Oatmeal can help you control your weight.

8. You probably already have oats in your kitchen.

7. Oatmeal may reduce the risk for type 2 diabetes.

6. Oats found in your grocery store are 100% natural.

5. Oatmeal may help reduce high blood pressure.

4. Oatmeal contains a wide array of vitamins, minerals and antioxidants and is a good source of protein, complex carbohydrates and iron.

3. Oatmeal may actually reduce the risk for certain cancers.

2. Oatmeal is quick and convenient.

1. Oatmeal can be absolutely delicious!

So have another Oatmeal cookie!

Peanut Butter Oatmeal Cookies SERVES 24 TO 30

There is no mistaking a peanut butter cookie when you see one. However, make no mistake, not all peanut butter cookies are created equal. Take a bite and see for yourself.

INGREDIENTS

⅔ cup .... pure olive oil
1 cup .... granulated sugar
1 cup .... dark brown sugar, packed
2 cups .... peanut butter
                       (natural is best)
2 teaspoons .... pure vanilla extract
1 large .... egg
3 large .... egg whites
3 tablespoons ...... milk
2 cups + 2 tbs ...... flour
2 cups .... quick oats
1 teaspoon .... baking soda
½ teaspoon .... salt
½ cup .... sugar, for rolling

PREPARATION

1. Preheat oven to 350°F. Lightly coat large cookie sheets with olive oil cooking spray.

2. In mixer bowl add olive oil, sugar, brown sugar, peanut butter, vanilla, egg, egg whites, and milk. Blend on medium speed until smooth and creamy.

3. Add flour, oats, baking soda, and salt. Blend well.

4. Roll dough into tablespoon size balls, or use a medium size cookie scoop. Roll in sugar. Place on prepared cookie sheets and press down twice (cross-way) with a fork.

5. Bake for 10~12 minutes. Cool on wire racks.

Coconuts About Weight Loss

My husband participated in a weight loss challenge at his work. He did fantastic as he lost 78 lbs in 4 months. Of course he bulked up for it and drank gallons of water before the weigh-in (haha). He decided that only raw foods were to be eaten before noon and there would be no mixing of carbohydrates and proteins at any time. He drove me nuts as he brought home GALLONS of virgin coconut oil that he said had to be used to cook with because it is a medium chain fat, does not store in your body as fat, and can convert to energy use. (I know all this because everyone we met got the infomercial version from him along with a mason jar of coconut oil to go.) Whoopee! I did not know as the weather got cooler that the coconut oil would harden. So how am I to pour it out of my cute spout bottles by the stove? It now looks like lard (yuck!). The up side is in the end he did win the contest along with $2,000. Normally I would be thrilled at such an accomplishment, but we had to use the money to pay off the year's supply of coconut oil we have in buckets all over our house. Anybody want some?

—Robin

Pecan Coconut Bars SERVES 9

These bars taste great with a generous scoop of vanilla ice cream or frozen yogurt. I am not a nut lover, but I am nuts about this recipe!

INGREDIENTS

½ cup.................. pure olive oil
2 cups .... brown sugar, packed
2 teaspoons .... pure vanilla extract
2 large .... eggs
1 large .... egg white
1 cup................... pecans, finely chopped
1 cup................... shredded coconut
1¾ cups .... flour
2 teaspoons .... baking powder
1 teaspoon.......... salt

PREPARATION

1. Preheat oven to 350°F. Coat one 9x9-inch pan with olive oil cooking spray.

2. In mixer bowl add olive oil, brown sugar, vanilla, eggs, and egg white. Blend on medium speed for 1~2 minutes or until smooth and creamy.

3. Add pecans and coconut. Mix until well blended.

4. Add flour, baking powder, and salt. Blend well.

5. Spread evenly in prepared pan and bake for 25~30 minutes or until a knife inserted into the center comes out clean.

Pink Frosted
Soft Sugar Cookies

Where I live almost every store sells these large, beautiful, soft sugar cookies. They are topped with pink frosting and colorful sprinkles. Locally, these cookies are famous! The problem is that they are filled with trans-fat. After playing in my kitchen and trying to make a cookie that would taste as great, and be better for you, I got it! You will enjoy this cookie with every pink bite.

INGREDIENTS

½ cup .... pure olive oil
1 cup .... vanilla yogurt
½ cup.................. granulated sugar
1 large .... egg
1 teaspoon .... pure vanilla extract
½ teaspoon .... butter extract
2¾ cups .... all purpose flour
1 teaspoon........... baking soda
½ teaspoon .... salt
1 Recipe Cream cheese frosting
Decorative sprinkles

PREPARATION

1. Preheat oven to 375°F. Coat cookie sheets with olive oil cooking spray.

2. In large mixer bowl add olive oil, yogurt, sugar, egg, and vanilla & butter extracts.

Mix on medium speed for 2 minutes or until smooth and creamy.

3. Add flour, baking soda, and salt. Mix on low speed until completely combined (dough should be a bit sticky).

4. Roll out onto a floured surface until dough is about ¼ inch thick.

5. Cut into desired shapes and place onto prepared cookie sheets.

6. Bake for 10~12 minutes. Cool completely and frost with Basic Cream Cheese Frosting (see page 32). Top with decorative sprinkles.

To turn the cream cheese frosting into a light pink color, add ¼ cup extra powdered sugar and 2~3 teaspoonfuls of cranberry juice or you could add a few drops of red food coloring.

Sneakerdoodles SERVES 26 TO 30

My Friend Roni makes the best snickerdoodles I have ever tasted. This recipe is a recreation of her recipe. Hi Roni!

INGREDIENTS

⅔ cup .... pure olive oil
1½ cup .... granulated sugar
2 large .... eggs
2 tablespoons ...... milk
1 teaspoon .... pure vanilla extract
½ teaspoon .... butter extract
2¾ cups .... flour
1 teaspoon .... baking soda
1½ teaspoons ...... cream of tartar
½ teaspoon .... salt

CINNAMON SUGAR
½ cup .... granulated sugar
1 teaspoon .... cinnamon

PREPARATION

1. Preheat oven to 375°F. Lightly coat large cookie sheets with olive oil cooking spray.

2. In mixer bowl add olive oil, sugar, eggs, milk, and vanilla & butter extracts. Blend until creamy.

3. Add flour, baking soda, cream of tartar, and salt. Blend until well mixed.

4. Roll dough into ping pong size balls. Roll in cinnamon sugar and place on prepared cookie sheets.

5. Bake for 8~10 minutes or until cookies are spread out and tops are light brown.

CINNAMON SUGAR PREPARATION
In small mixing bowl, add sugar and cinnamon. Mix until combined.

Soft Ginger Roos serves 48 to 54

This recipe use to be called "Soft Ginger Snaps", but a darling British friend named Carol said that she liked the "Ginger Roos." It sounded so cute that I renamed them.

INGREDIENTS

1 cup.................... pure olive oil
2 cups .... brown sugar, packed
2 large .... eggs
½ cup................... molasses
2 teaspoons .... pure vanilla extract
1 teaspoon.......... butter extract
4½ cups .... flour
4 teaspoons .... baking soda
¾ teaspoon.......... salt
1½ teaspoons ...... fresh minced or
                        ground ginger
2 teaspoons .... cinnamon
1 teaspoon.......... cloves
¾ cup.................. granulated sugar for rolling

PREPARATION

1. Preheat oven to 375°F. Lightly coat large cookie sheets with olive oil cooking spray.

2. In mixer bowl combine olive oil, brown sugar, eggs, molasses, and vanilla & butter extracts. Blend until smooth and creamy.

3. Add flour, baking soda, salt, ginger, cinnamon, and cloves. Mix until well blended.

4. Roll dough into small teaspoon size balls, or use a small cookie scoop. Roll in sugar and place on prepared cookie sheets.

5. Bake for 7~10 minutes. Remove and let cool on cookie sheets for 5 minutes.

For a smaller batch, this recipe can be cut in half.

Molasses Tidbit: *When a recipe calls for molasses or honey and oil, I measure the oil first and pour it out. Then I measure the molasses or honey in the same cup. It flows out without sticking, because the inside of the measuring cup is still slightly "oiled."*

Muffins
& Sweet Breads

Almond-Lemon Poppy Seed Bread SERVES 16 TO 20

An old time sweet bread with a little zest! Remember to check your teeth before you flash a smile.

INGREDIENTS

⅔ cup .... pure olive oil
1 large .... egg
2 large .... egg whites
1½ cups .... low fat milk
2¼ cups .... granulated sugar
2½ tablespoons ... lemon zest
1 large .... lemon, juiced
2 teaspoons .... pure vanilla extract
½ teaspoon .... almond extract
3 cups .... all purpose flour
2 teaspoons .... baking powder
1 teaspoon .... salt
2 tablespoons ...... poppy seeds

LEMON GLAZE

2 cups .... powdered sugar
⅓ cup .... fresh lemon juice
1 teaspoon .... pure vanilla extract
1 teaspoon .... almond extract
½ cup .... thinly sliced almonds

PREPARATION

1. Preheat oven to 350°F. Coat two 9x5-inch loaf pans with olive oil cooking spray.

2. In mixer bowl add olive oil, egg, egg whites, milk, sugar, lemon zest, lemon juice, and vanilla & almond extracts. Blend on medium speed for 2 minutes or until creamy.

3. Add flour, baking powder, salt, and poppy seeds. Mix until moistened.

4. Pour into prepared loaf pans and bake for 55~60 minutes or until a knife inserted into the center comes out clean. Remove from oven and cool on wire racks.

LEMON GLAZE PREPARATION
In mixing bowl add powdered sugar, lemon juice, vanilla & almond extracts. Mix until well blended. While hot, pour lemon glaze evenly over loaves and sprinkle almonds on top. Serve warm or cold.

Banana Bread SERVES 12 TO 15

I love to make banana bread. The riper the bananas, the sweeter they taste. I have used them when the peels were turning black and they work even better. To add a unique twist to this recipe, try shredding a little bit of dark chocolate candy bar into the mix.

INGREDIENTS

1¾ cups .... brown sugar, packed
2 large .... eggs
2 large .... egg whites
½ cup.................. pure olive oil
1½ teaspoons ...... pure vanilla extract
2 medium .... extra ripe bananas, mashed
½ cup.................. vanilla yogurt
2 cups .... flour
2 teaspoons .... baking powder
½ teaspoon.......... baking soda
1 teaspoon........... salt
½ teaspoon.......... cinnamon
½ teaspoon.......... nutmeg

PREPARATION

1. Preheat oven to 350°F. Generously coat one large or two small loaf baking pans with olive oil cooking spray.

2. In mixer bowl add brown sugar, eggs, egg whites, olive oil, and vanilla. Beat on medium speed for 2 minutes.

3. Add bananas and yogurt. Blend for another minute.

4. Add flour, baking powder, baking soda, salt, cinnamon, and nutmeg. Blend until smooth. Pour into prepared loaf pans.

5. Bake for 45~55 minutes or until a knife inserted into the center comes out clean.

This recipe can be doubled.

BANANA TIDBIT: *Many times we have an abundance of over ripe bananas. Next time, try puréeing them in the blender, put them in a plastic freezer bag, mark it with the number of bananas puréed and put it in the freezer. That way, the next time you want to bake banana bread you will have it handy. It takes only seconds in the microwave to defrost and you are good to go.*

Blueberry Streusel Serves 8

This is a coffee cake turned streusel with the added super food, blueberries!!!

INGREDIENTS

⅓ cup .... pure olive oil
½ cup.................. granulated sugar
2 large .... egg whites
1 large .... egg
⅓ cup .... milk
1 teaspoon........... pure vanilla extract
1½ cups .... flour
2 teaspoons .... baking powder
½ teaspoon.......... salt
1 cup.................... frozen blueberries

Topping
6 tablespoons...... flour
6 tablespoons...... powdered sugar
½ teaspoon.......... cinnamon
dash.................... salt
3 tablespoons...... pure olive oil

Glaze
1 cup.................... powdered sugar
4 teaspoons .... water

PREPARATION

1. Preheat oven to 375°F. Coat one 9-inch round or one 8-inch square baking pan with olive oil cooking spray.

2. In mixing bowl, blend together (by hand) olive oil, sugar, egg whites, egg, milk, and vanilla.

3. In medium size mixing bowl combine; flour, baking powder, and salt.

4. Fold frozen blueberries into flour mixture and toss until well coated.

5. Fold flour/blueberry mixture into moistened ingredients until just mixed.

6. Pour into prepared pan and sprinkle with streusel topping. Bake for 35~45 minutes or until a knife inserted into the center comes out clean.

Topping Preparation
In small mixing bowl add flour, powdered sugar, cinnamon, salt, and olive oil.

Glaze Preparation
In small mixing bowl add powdered sugar and water. Blend until mixed. When streusel is ready, remove from oven and drizzle glaze on top while still hot.

Chocolate Chip Banana Crumble Muffins

SERVES 12

Wondering what to do with all those overripe bananas? Try this recipe and you will know what to do every time.

INGREDIENTS

¼ cup................... pure olive oil
1 large .... egg, beaten
3 medium .... bananas, mashed
¾ cup................... granulated sugar
1 teaspoon........... pure vanilla extract
1½ cups .... flour
1 teaspoon........... baking soda
1 teaspoon........... baking powder
½ teaspoon.......... salt
½ cup.................. mini chocolate chips

CRUMBLE TOPPING
⅓ cup .... packed brown sugar
3 tablespoons...... all-purpose flour
¼ teaspoon......... cinnamon
2 tablespoons ..... pure olive oil

PREPARATION

1. Preheat oven to 375°F. Line 12 muffin tins with paper liners and generously spray with olive oil cooking spray.

2. In mixer bowl add olive oil, egg, bananas, sugar, and vanilla. Blend until smooth and creamy.

3. In separate mixing bowl, add 1½ cups flour, baking soda, baking powder and salt.

4. Fold flour mixture into moistened ingredients. Blend until just mixed. Gently fold in chocolate chips.

5. Fill muffin tins ⅔ full and sprinkle each muffin with about a teaspoon of the topping mix.

6. Bake for 15~20 minutes, or until a toothpick inserted into center of a muffin comes out clean.

TOPPING PREPARATION
In a small bowl, mix together brown sugar, flour and cinnamon. Add olive oil and cut with a fork. The topping will resemble coarse meal.

Bananas When I was a little boy, I was traveling in a train along a mountain pass with my grandfather, who had packed some food for our journey. He unpacked the food and handed me a banana. I was hungry, so I quickly accepted it and took a bite. It so happened that at the moment I took the bite the train entered a long tunnel and everything went pitch black. I screamed, "I'm blind!" After what seemed like a very long two minutes or so with my Grandfather comforting me, we exited the tunnel and my "vision" came back. I seriously thought I had gone blind, and because I was eating the banana at the time I assumed it caused my blindness.

Ever since the train trip with my grandfather, I haven't eaten bananas. Even now, when my wife makes her delicious banana pudding, which all my kids and grandkids love, I won't eat any for fear of becoming blind again.

—LeRoy

I say, seize the moment. Remember all those women on the Titanic who waved off the dessert cart.

—Erma Bombeck

The War of the Twisties

We ladies do have an ego when it comes to our special recipes. Off and on through the years my husband's work has taken us to Japan. We lived in Tokyo and were surrounded by a large group of gaijin (foreigners to Japan). There we attended a church which has a large women's organization. One day I went to a baby shower and tasted some incredible cinnamon twists. I asked who made them and my friend Kira (name changed) said that she made up the recipe and that it was fashioned from a quick breadstick recipe from another friend of mine named Lois (named changed). Then the war began. A church cookbook was being organized and everyone was to submit their prized recipes. Many ladies submitted the Cinnamon Twists recipe and called it their own. We had moved back to the States by then, but I understand that working out the twists recipe was a big ordeal. I'm not going to say who made it into the cookbook, but I will say this – "Step aside ladies, because it's my recipe now!" Hahaha!

—Micki

Cinnamon Twisties

There are many ways to make cinnamon rolls. This recipe is a simple and quick way to make yet another version of these old time classics.

INGREDIENTS

⅓ cup .... pure olive oil
1½ cups .... warm water 110°F ~ 115°F
                  (baby bottle warm)
1 tablespoon .... instant dry yeast
4 cups .... all purpose flour
1 teaspoon .... salt
½ cup.................. granulated sugar
1 teaspoon .... pure vanilla extract
1 large .... egg

CINNAMON SUGAR
½~¾ cup .... granulated sugar
1 tablespoon .... cinnamon

EASY GLAZE
2 cups .... powdered sugar
⅓ cup .... evaporated milk
1 teaspoon .... pure vanilla extract
1 pinch .... salt

PREPARATION

1. Preheat oven to 400°F. Pour olive oil onto a large jelly roll pan and spread evenly to coat the entire pan. Set aside.

2. Proof yeast by mixing ½ cup of the warm water with a tablespoon of sugar and yeast. Let stand 5 minutes.

3. Combine remaining water with flour, salt, sugar, vanilla, and egg.

4. Add yeast/water mixture to flour mixture and knead by mixer or by hand. When dough is smooth and elastic, roll out onto a well floured surface. Shape into a large rectangle (just smaller than a jelly roll pan).

5. Using a pizza cutter, cut in half lengthwise, then slice widthwise by 1~1½ inch strips. Twist strips and place side by side in prepared pan, leaving about ¼~½ inch between strips. Bottoms of twisties will be coated with olive oil. Flip the twisties over. Evenly sprinkle each twist with about a teaspoon of cinnamon/sugar (some of the cinnamon/sugar will fall into pan, that's okay).

6. Cover with plastic and let rise until double in size (40~60 minutes).

7. Bake for 10~12 minutes or until tops are golden brown. While still hot, drizzle with glaze mixture.

GLAZE PREPARATION
In small mixing bowl, add powdered sugar, evaporated milk, vanilla, and salt. Blend until completely mixed.

Co-Co's Amazing Bran Muffins

SERVES 50 TO 60

My cute neighbor Collette, aka Co-Co, made these wonderful bran muffins for me one day and I loved them so much I adapted them just a bit. The best thing about this recipe is that you make one large batch and use as much as you need. It keeps in the refrigerator for 6 weeks!

INGREDIENTS

2 cups .... boiling hot water
4 cups .... all-bran cereal
5 teaspoons .... baking soda
2 cups .... granulated sugar
⅔ cup .... pure olive oil
2 teaspoons .... pure vanilla extract
½ teaspoon .... butter extract
1 quart .... buttermilk
2 cups .... 40% bran flakes
5 cups .... flour
1 teaspoon .... salt

PREPARATION

1. Preheat oven to 400°F. Line muffin tins with paper liners or coat with olive oil cooking spray.

2. In a medium size mixing bowl, add boiling water, all-bran, and baking soda. Mix until all ingredients are moistened and set aside.

3. And in a large mixing bowl add sugar, olive oil, vanilla & butter extracts, buttermilk, and bran flakes. Blend together until well mixed.

4. Add water/bran mixture and blend. Fold in flour and salt, mixing until completely moistened.

5. Fill muffin tins ⅔ full and bake for 15~20 minutes. Cool on wire racks.

Converted Scones

The first scones were said to have originated in Scotland and date back to a time (1600s) when Scottish Kings were crowned. The original scone was triangle shaped, made of oats, and griddle fried. This scone recipe is converted from an old Utah pioneer recipe. Some love them baked, some love them fried. You choose. Either way, this is one great treat everyone will love time and time again.

INGREDIENTS

½ cup .... warm water 110°F ~ 115°F
(baby bottle warm)
1 tablespoon .... instant dry yeast
1 teaspoon .... granulated sugar
4½ cups .... all purpose flour
¼ cup .... granulated sugar
1 teaspoon .... salt
¼ cup .... pure olive oil
1 large .... egg
1 cup .... buttermilk (room temperature)
1½ teaspoons ...... pure vanilla extract

PREPARATION

1. Coat two large cookie sheets with olive oil. Set aside.

2. In a small non-metallic bowl add water, yeast and a teaspoon of sugar. Set aside and allow to proof (about 2 minutes).

3. In a large mixing bowl, add 3 cups of flour, sugar, and salt. Mix until combined and set aside.

4. In a mixer bowl add olive oil, egg, buttermilk, and vanilla. Mix on medium speed and begin adding yeast mixture until well blended.

5. Add flour mixture and blend again. At this point the dough will be sticky. Using a dough hook, mix on medium speed and slowly to add remaining flour in ¼ ~ ½ cup measurements. Knead on medium speed for 6~8 minutes or until the dough is smooth and elastic.

6. Pour a couple of teaspoonfuls of olive oil in a medium size mixing bowl and place the dough inside, turning once to coat. Cover and let rise until double in bulk (about one hour).

7. Punch down and divide dough into 20~24 balls. On a floured surface, roll into golf ball size, oval shapes.

8. Place on prepared cookie sheets. Cover and let rise for 30 minutes.

For Baking: Pre-heat oven to 375°F. Lightly brush scone tops with olive oil. Bake for 15~20 minutes or until golden brown.

For Frying: Pour about 1½~2 inches of pure olive oil in a 12~18 inch frying pan. Heat on medium. Place about 6 scones into pan and fry until each side is golden brown. Remove and place on paper towels. Serve hot with jam or honey.

SPRAY REPLACEMENT TIDBIT: *If you should decide to coat the entire pan with pure olive oil rather than cooking spray, pour olive oil into a small dish and use a pastry brush to coat entire pan.*

Craisin Muffins SERVES 12

This is a great dessert muffin, but I think it is a delicious muffin to wake up to anytime.

INGREDIENTS

1 large .... egg, beaten
½ cup................... buttermilk
⅓ cup .... pure olive oil
½ cup................... granulated sugar (plus a bit
                                  extra for the muffin tops)
1 teaspoon........... lemon zest
1 whole .... lemon, squeezed
1 teaspoon........... pure vanilla extract
1½ cups .... flour
2 teaspoons .... baking powder
¾ teaspoon.......... salt
½ cup................... Craisins (or raisins)

PREPARATION

1. Heat oven to 400°F. Line 12 muffin tins with paper liners or generously coat with olive oil cooking spray.

2. In mixer bowl add egg, buttermilk, olive oil, sugar, lemon zest, lemon juice, and vanilla. Mix by hand until well blended.

3. Add flour, baking powder, and salt. Mix until just moistened. Batter will be lumpy and moist.

4. Fold in Craisins and fill muffin cups ⅔ full. Sprinkle tops with sugar.

5. Bake for 15~18 minutes or until top springs back when touched and the muffins are golden brown. Remove from pan immediately. Cool on wire racks.

Dad's Apple Cinnamon Rolls

SERVES 26 TO 30

My Dad sent me a sweet story about himself as a small child in the 1940s, baking with his grandmother in the kitchen. This recipe was inspired by that story.

INGREDIENTS

2 cups .... milk, scalded and cooled
¼ cup................... pure olive oil
½ cup................... granulated sugar
1½ teaspoons ...... salt
5~6 cups.............. all purpose flour
1 tablespoon .... instant dry yeast
1 medium .... apple, peeled and finely chopped

FILLING
2 tablespoons...... pure olive oil
½ small box......... instant vanilla pudding (dry)
⅓ cup.................. granulated sugar
1 tablespoon .... cinnamon
½ teaspoon.......... nutmeg

PREPARATION

1. Preheat oven to 400°F. Coat one 9x13 pan with olive oil or olive oil cooking spray.

2. Scald milk and pour into a large mixing bowl and cool until lukewarm, 110°~115°F (baby bottle warm).

3. Add olive oil, sugar, salt, half of the flour, and yeast. Mix together until well blended.

4. Fold in apples. Let mixture stand for 10 minutes and allow to cool until lukewarm.

5. Add remaining flour (reserving one cup). Mix until blended. Pour out onto a large floured surface. Lightly knead the dough, adding reserved cup of flour as needed until the dough is no longer sticky. While working with the dough, continue to add small amounts of flour until the dough becomes smooth and elastic. Roll out into a rectangular shape (about ½ inch thick).

6. Evenly spread 2 tablespoons of olive oil over the surface of the dough. Sprinkle prepared filling over dough, covering entire surface.

7. Roll the dough length-wise and tightly pinch the edges to seal. Using string or dental floss, cut into ½ inch slices. Place on baking sheets and let rise until double in size.

8. Bake for 15~20 minutes or until tops are brown. Cool and frost with basic cream cheese frosting. (see page 32)

FILLING PREPARATION
In small mixing bowl add dry pudding, sugar, cinnamon, and nutmeg. Mix together.

Queen Clara Belle

My grandmother was one of the greatest bread bakers of all time. As she grew older, she became diabetic and eventually became blind as a result of this malady. But Grandma Clara Belle was not one to quit doing what she really loved.

One morning, when I was about 10, she came to me and asked if I would help her select the ingredients for that week's baking. To say I was honored would be a gross understatement. After all, I was just a kid, and a boy at that, and I was being asked to take part in a ritual that (in my mind) was the domain of a queen. It wasn't until much later that I learned that she was, in fact, almost totally blind.

After I had helped her obtain and arrange all of the ingredients and implements for the day's cooking, I was allowed to watch as she worked the entire day in the kitchen, moving from counter to table to sink in a purposeful dance. There was never a missed step, and somehow the temperature of the oven was always perfect for whatever she was baking: dinner rolls, pudgy but light loaves of white bread, shamrock rolls (a special treat just for our lunch) and cinnamon rolls. I even got to help mix and spread the cinnamon-and-sugar filling on the pie shaped dough which was then rolled. The rolls were then cut into inch-and-a-half rounds and baked for what was probably only about ten or twelve minutes, but seemed like hours.

To this day, I cannot be in a house where fresh cinnamon rolls are being made without being taken back to that Wisconsin kitchen in the mid-1940s where I imagine, with my eyes closed, that I have once again been permitted to be a servant to Queen Clara Belle.

—Dad

Double Dutch Chocolate Chip Muffins

It's all about the chocolate, and it's all chocolate!

INGREDIENTS

½ cup................... dark brown sugar
½ cup................... granulated sugar
2 large .... eggs
1 cup................... milk
½ cup.................. pure olive oil
2 teaspoons .... pure vanilla extract
1¾ cups .... flour
½ cup .... cocoa (Dutch milled is best)
2 teaspoons .... baking powder
½ teaspoon.......... salt
1 cup................... semisweet or milk chocolate
                         chips (reserve ¼ cup)

CHOCOLATE CRUMB TOPPING
½ cup................... granulated sugar
2 tablespoons...... flour
2 tablespoons...... cocoa
2 tablespoons...... pure olive oil
¼ cup.................. reserved chocolate chips

PREPARATION

1. Preheat oven to 375°F. Line 12 muffin tins with paper liners or generously coat with olive oil cooking spray.

2. In a mixer bowl add sugars, eggs, milk, olive oil, and vanilla. Mix on medium speed until well blended.

3. Add flour, cocoa, baking powder, and salt. Blend by hand until just moistened.

4. Gently fold in ¾ cup of the chocolate chips. Do not overmix.

5. Evenly pour batter into prepared muffin tins. Evenly spoon a teaspoonful of crumb topping onto each muffin.

6. Bake for 20~25 minutes or until a knife inserted into center comes out clean. Cool at least 5 minutes.

CHOCOLATE CRUMB TOPPING PREPARATION
In a small mixing bowl add sugar, flour, cocoa, and olive oil. Blend with a fork until mixture resembles coarse meal. Mix in remaining chocolate chips.

Fresh Blueberry Muffins

Beautiful 9-year old Sable was visiting my home with her parents when I made these muffins for dessert one evening. She loved them so much that she asked me to e-mail her the recipe so that she could make them for her family. I was happy to help this young baking enthusiast, so I sent the recipe the next day.

INGREDIENTS

2 cups	flour
½ cup	quick oats
¾ cup	powdered sugar
2 teaspoons	baking powder
½ teaspoon	baking soda
½ teaspoon	salt
1 cup	vanilla yogurt
½ cup	pure olive oil
1 teaspoon	lemon zest
1 teaspoon	pure vanilla extract
2 large	eggs
1 cup	fresh or frozen blueberries

OPTIONAL CRUMBLE TOPPING

¼ cup	quick oats
⅓ cup	brown sugar
2 tablespoons	pure olive oil
1 pinch	salt

LEMON GLAZE TOPPING

1 cup	powdered sugar
2 tablespoons	fresh lemon juice
½ teaspoon	pure vanilla extract
1 pinch	salt

PREPARATION

1. Preheat oven to 400°F. Line 12 muffin or 32 mini muffin tins with paper liners or generously coat with olive oil cooking spray.

2. In a large mixing bowl add flour, oats, powdered sugar, baking powder, baking soda, and salt. Stir until well blended.

3. In a medium size mixing bowl combine yogurt, olive oil, lemon zest, vanilla, and eggs. Blend well by hand.

4. Add to dry ingredients and blend until just moistened. Gently fold in blueberries. Fill muffin tins ¾ full.

5. Bake for 15~20 minutes (12~15 minutes for mini). Remove from oven and cool for 5 minutes. Remove muffins from tins and cool completely on wire racks.

CRUMB TOPPING PREPARATION

In small mixing bowl combine oats, brown sugar, olive oil, and salt.

LEMON GLAZE TOPPING PREPARATION

In a small plastic zip bag add powdered sugar, lemon juice, vanilla, and salt. Remove air and tightly seal bag. Massage bag until glaze is well mixed. Cut a small hole in the corner of the plastic zip bag and with a back and forth motion, glaze the top of each muffin.

The Best Vanilla Ever

I am always giving my fancy friends a hard time about how much money they spend on their clothes. Especially how much they will spend on a pair of jeans. Did you know that there are jeans that cost $175? I was blown away. I said "How could anyone spend that much on a pair of jeans?"

The answer came, "you just have to try them on and you will see why they are the best jeans ever." I just teased my friends and told them that I was simply not that extravagant.

Well, one day I was teaching a cooking class and I was explaining that the vanilla I was using was the very best vanilla that you could possibly buy. One student asked, "How much is that vanilla?" My answer, without thinking twice, was "$15." They responded, "You would spend $15 on that small bottle of vanilla?!" And it hit me…. I'm a snob – a food snob… a vanilla snob.

Yes, I admit it. But I still won't pay $175 for a pair of jeans.

Silly how we all are.

—Micki

Ginger Bread
SERVES 14 TO 16

This is a Christmas favorite but I find it to be a hit anytime of year.

INGREDIENTS

½ cup	pure olive oil
½ cup	brown sugar (packed)
1 large	egg, beaten
1 cup	molasses
1 tablespoon	milk
1 teaspoon	pure vanilla extract
2½ cups	flour
1½ teaspoons	baking soda
½ teaspoon	salt
1 teaspoon	cinnamon
½ teaspoon	ground ginger
1 teaspoon	ground cloves
1 cup	very hot water

GLAZE

1½ cups	powdered sugar
4 tablespoons	milk
1 pinch	salt

PREPARATION

1. Preheat oven to 350°F. Generously coat one bundt cake pan with olive oil cooking spray.

2. In mixer bowl add olive oil, brown sugar, and egg. Blend until smooth and creamy.

3. Add molasses, milk, and vanilla. Mix until well blended. Add flour, baking soda, salt, cinnamon, ginger, and cloves. Blend until well mixed.

4. Slowly add hot water and mix on low speed, scraping sides if necessary until well blended. Pour into prepared bundt pan.

5. Bake for 40~45 minutes or until a knife inserted into the center comes out clean. Remove from oven and let cool in pan for 5 minutes.

6. Remove from pan and place in the center of a large plate. Glaze while still hot. Serve with bananas and whipped cream.

GLAZE PREPARATION
In a small mixing bowl combine powdered sugar, milk, and salt. Blend until completely mixed.

Johnny Apple Bread

When Johnny went around planting all those apple seeds, he never knew the possibilities.

INGREDIENTS

¾ cup................... pure olive oil
1 large .... egg
2 large .... egg whites
½ cup................... fat free vanilla yogurt
2 cups .... dark brown sugar, packed
2 teaspoons .... pure vanilla extract
2½ cups .... flour
½ teaspoon.......... baking powder
1 teaspoon........... baking soda
1 teaspoon........... salt
1 teaspoon........... cinnamon
½ cup................... quick oats
2½ cups .... apples, peeled and finely
                 chopped

CINNAMON SUGAR
4 tablespoons...... granulated sugar
1 teaspoon........... cinnamon

PREPARATION

1. Preheat oven to 350°F. Coat 2 medium size bread loaf pans with olive oil cooking spray.

2. In mixer bowl add olive oil, egg, egg whites, yogurt, brown sugar, and vanilla. On medium speed, blend until smooth.

3. Add flour, baking powder, baking soda, and salt. Blend until well mixed.

4. Add quick oats and blend again.

5. Fold in apples and pour into prepared loaf pans. Sprinkle cinnamon sugar on top.

6. Bake for 45~55 minutes or until a knife inserted into the center comes out clean. Cool in pan for 5~10 minutes. Remove from pan and cool on wire rack.

CINNAMON SUGAR PREPARATION
In small mixing bowl, combine sugar and cinnamon.

Peach Crumble Muffins

SERVES 12~14

If the state of Georgia had an official state muffin, this would be it.

INGREDIENTS

¼ cup.................. pure olive oil
¾ cup.................. granulated sugar
1 large .... egg
2 large .... egg whites
1 teaspoon.......... pure vanilla extract
1½ cups .... flour
1 teaspoon.......... baking soda
½ teaspoon.......... salt
½ teaspoon.......... cinnamon
1 cup.................. fresh, canned (drained) or
                     frozen peaches (thawed and
                     diced)

STREUSEL TOPPING
½ cup.................. brown sugar, packed
½ cup.................. flour
1 teaspoon.......... pure vanilla extract
3 tablespoons...... pure olive oil

PREPARATION

1. Preheat oven to 350°F. Line muffin tins with paper liners or coat with olive oil cooking spray.

2. In medium size mixing bowl add olive oil, sugar, egg, egg whites, and vanilla. Mix until smooth and creamy.

3. Add flour, baking soda, salt, and cinnamon. Blend until just moistened. Gently fold in peaches.

4. Fill muffin tins ⅔ full and spoon streusel on top. Bake for 20~25 minutes or until brown and firm to the touch. Remove from oven and cool on wire racks.

STREUSEL PREPARATION
Mix brown sugar and flour together. Cut in vanilla and oil. Blend until mixture is crumbly.

Pies & Crisps

Chapter 4

All American Apple Pie

Now all you need is a hot dog and a Chevrolet.

INGREDIENTS

1 recipe .... Perfect Olive Oil Pie Crust
(see page 130)
5 cups .... tart apples, peeled
and chopped
1 teaspoon........... pure vanilla extract
1 cup................... granulated sugar
1 teaspoon........... cinnamon
½ teaspoon.......... nutmeg
1 teaspoon........... lemon zest
2 tablespoons...... all purpose flour
1 tablespoon .... pure olive oil

PREPARATION

1. Preheat oven to 400°F. Prepare top and bottom of perfect olive oil pie crust.

2. In a large mixing bowl combine all ingredients and blend well.

3. Pour into prepared pie shell. Assemble top crust, pinch edges together to seal. Slice small holes in the crust for ventilation.

4. Brush with egg wash (see page 130) and sprinkle sugar on top. Place pie plate onto a large cookie sheet (to catch any running juices).

5. Bake for 15 minutes. Reduce temperature to 350°F and without opening oven door, bake for another 45 minutes. Remove and let cool for 30~45 minutes. Serve with light vanilla ice cream or frozen yogurt.

BROWN BAGGING IT TIDBIT: *Try placing your apple pie in a large brown paper bag. Fold the top of the bag over a few inches, staple the top and bake according to directions. This helps to give the top crust a nice firm texture, while allowing the bottom crust to brown up nicely.*

Homemade Spaghetti Bars

When I was in college I visited my sister for the weekend, I walked into the kitchen where she was feeding her three small children and asked one of them "whatcha eaten?" Being only three years old, he said "pasgetti bars, Aunti." I said "Neeto". I told my sister that was kind of clever to make bars out of the spaghetti. She replied, "What do you mean, clever? That's just how it always turns out." I said, "Ever heard of olive oil in the pot?" She said, "olive oil? What for?" Her children, now grown, still come home for homemade spaghetti bars that they can't get anywhere else but in Mom's kitchen.

—Robin

When women are depressed,
they either eat or go shopping.
Men invade another country:
It's a whole different way
of thinking.

—Elaine Boosler

Any Berry Pie Serves 10 to 12

This pie works great with any kind of berry. Pick your favorite berry, and then call this your berry favorite pie.

INGREDIENTS

1 recipe	Perfect Olive Oil Pie Crust (see page 130)
1 cup	granulated sugar
½ cup	all purpose flour
¾ teaspoon	cinnamon
2 teaspoons	pure vanilla extract
1 teaspoon	orange zest
½ tablespoon	salt
4 cups	frozen berries, any type
2 tablespoons	pure olive oil

PREPARATION

1. Preheat oven to 425°F. Prepare top and bottom of perfect olive oil pie crust.

2. In mixing bowl add sugar, flour, cinnamon, vanilla, orange zest, and salt.

3. Add berries into flour mixture and toss until well coated. Let stand for 15 minutes.

4. Pour mixture into prepared pie shell.

5. Drizzle olive oil evenly over berries. Assemble top crust, pinch edges together to seal and slice small holes in the crust for ventilation.

6. Brush with egg wash (see page 130) and sprinkle sugar on top.

7. Bake for 15 minutes. Reduce heat to 350°F and without opening oven door, bake for another 40~45 minutes. Serve piping hot with vanilla bean ice cream.

There is no love sincerer than the love of food.

—George Bernard Shaw

Corn Flake Pie Crust

My sister-in-law Penny cannot have wheat of any kind. I developed this pie crust for her and all of her friends in the Celiac's club.

INGREDIENTS

4 cups .... corn flakes, crushed
2 tablespoons ...... brown sugar
1 pinch .... salt
3 tablespoons ...... honey
3 tablespoons ...... pure olive oil

PREPARATION

1. Preheat oven to 350°F.

2. In a mixing bowl, combine crushed corn flakes, brown sugar, salt, and olive oil.

3. Press mixture evenly and firmly into bottom and up sides of a 9-inch pie plate.

4. Bake for 10 minutes or until lightly browned. Cool completely.

Graham Cracker Crust Yields 1 Crust

What can I say? It's graham cracker crust only better for you!

INGREDIENTS

2 cups .... crushed graham crackers
½ teaspoon .... cinnamon
4 tablespoons ...... honey
1 large .... egg white
⅓ cup .... pure olive oil

PREPARATION

1. Mix all ingredients with a fork until evenly moistened.

2. Gently press crust into an 8~9 inch pie pan.

3. Bake according to recipe instructions.

Large Eggs   My husband doesn't help in the kitchen much, but he's always willing to pick things up at the store for me. I learned early in my marriage that I need to be VERY specific when I write my shopping lists for him.

Once when I needed a carton of large eggs, I had hastily written "L eggs" on the list. Much to my dismay, however, there were no eggs in the shopping bag when he returned. I quickly forgave him though when he triumphantly stated that he had gotten everything on the list —even the pantyhose!

—Lori

Lemon Meringue Pie SERVES 10 TO 12

This fresh pie takes little time to prepare. After just one taste they will think you have spent hours. That will be our little secret.

INGREDIENTS

1 recipe	Graham Cracker Crust (see page 122)
4 medium	egg yolks
1⅓ cups	granulated sugar
⅓ cup	cornstarch
1½ cups	water
¼ teaspoon	salt
3 tablespoons	pure olive oil
½ cup	fresh lemon juice
1 tablespoon	lemon zest
1 teaspoon	pure vanilla extract

MERINGUE

6 medium	egg whites
¼ teaspoon	cream of tartar
3 tablespoons	sugar

PREPARATION

1. Adjust the oven rack to the middle position and preheat oven to 375°F.

2. In medium size mixing bowl, beat egg yolks until smooth. Set aside.

3. In a medium saucepan, combine cornstarch, water, sugar, and salt. Whisk to combine. Over medium heat, while constantly stirring, bring mixture to a boil for about 1 minute.

4. Remove from heat and slowly add cornstarch mixture into the mixing bowl with the egg yolk mixture. Pour blended mixture back into the pan and while stirring, warm over medium heat for about 1 minute.

5. Remove from heat. Add olive oil, lemon juice, zest, and vanilla. Mix until well blended. Pour mixture into prepared pie shell and top with meringue. Make sure meringue completely covers filling.

6. Bake on center rack for 10~12 minutes or until meringue is golden brown in color. Remove from oven and cool in refrigerator 4-6 hours before slicing.

MERINGUE TOPPING PREPARATION

1. Place egg whites in mixer bowl.

2. Using a whisk attachment, beat egg whites until soft peaks form.

3. Gradually add sugar and cream of tartar. Continue beating until stiff peaks form, approximately 1½~2 minutes.

FRESH EGG TIDBIT: *Fill a bowl or pan with cold water. Place the egg in the water. If it sinks to the bottom, it is fresh. If the egg rises to the top, the egg is no good. Save yourself a tummy ache if you are unsure when you last bought your eggs! This is an especially good tip if you are a cookie dough eater.*

Peach Cobbler SERVES 8 TO 10

I love cobbler, especially during a campout, when baked in a Dutch oven. It is a little like a peach cake with a crunchy top. With a subtle taste of cinnamon baked in, this cobbler tastes like summer.

INGREDIENTS

1 small can .... sliced peaches (15 oz)
                      (reserve ½ cup juice)
⅓ cup .... pure olive oil
⅓ cup .... granulated sugar
1 teaspoon .... pure vanilla extract
½ teaspoon .... cinnamon
1 large .... egg
1 cup.................... all purpose flour
2 teaspoons .... baking powder
¼ teaspoon.......... salt

PREPARATION

1. Preheat oven to 350°F. Lightly coat medium size casserole dish with olive oil cooking spray.

2. In mixing bowl add ½ cup reserved peach juice, olive oil, sugar, vanilla, cinnamon, and egg. Blend on medium for 1 minute.

3. Add flour, baking powder, and salt. Blend until smooth.

4. Pour batter into prepared pan. Place peaches on top of batter. For added sweetness sprinkle with a tablespoon of sugar.

5. Bake for 45~55 minutes. When top is brown, remove from oven and serve piping hot with peach ice cream.

Pecan Pie SERVES 8 TO 10

Our 90-year-old Grandfather lives in Arkansas and brought us fresh pecans that he picked and shelled himself. What a treat! The fresher the better. But with pecans from anywhere, you cannot go wrong with this pie.

INGREDIENTS

1 recipe .... Perfect Olive Oil Pie Crust
      (see page 130)
1 large .... egg, beaten
3 large .... egg whites, beaten
½ cup.................. brown sugar, packed
½ teaspoon.......... salt
1 cup................... light corn syrup
1 tablespoon .... pure olive oil
1 teaspoon........... pure vanilla extract
1 teaspoon.......... butter extract
1½ cups .... pecans (whole or chopped)

PREPARATION

1. Preheat oven to 375°F. Prepare perfect olive oil pie crust (uses bottom crust only).

2. In mixer bowl add egg, egg whites, brown sugar, salt, corn syrup, olive oil, and vanilla & butter extracts. Blend on medium speed until smooth.

3. Fold in pecans. Spoon into prepared un-baked pie crust.

4. Bake for 15 minutes. Reduce temperature to 325°F and without opening oven door, bake for an additional 35~40 minutes, or until a knife inserted into the center comes out clean.

This recipe can be doubled to fill both shells.

Perfect Olive Oil
Pie Crust YIELDS 1~2 PIECE PIE CRUST

Oil pie crusts are notorious for being difficult to work with. After much experimenting, this crust came out perfect. It is the simplest pie crust you will ever make. It bakes up light and crispy.

INGREDIENTS

2½ cups .... all purpose flour, sifted
1 tablespoon .... granulated sugar
1 teaspoon .... salt
½ cup .... pure olive oil
⅔ cup .... buttermilk
1 teaspoon .... pure vanilla extract

EGG WASH
1 medium .... egg white
2 teaspoons .... cold water

PREPARATION

1. In mixing bowl add flour, sugar, and salt. Mix together.

2. Add olive oil, buttermilk, and vanilla. Using a spatula, blend all ingredients. If necessary, add a sprinkle of flour to create desired texture; not too wet and not too dry.

3. Divide dough into 2 equal parts. Form balls and wrap individually in plastic wrap. Flatten with the palm of your hand. Let rest for 5~10 minutes (no need to refrigerate).

4. Roll out between wax or parchment paper. Assemble pie according to recipe instructions.

EGG WASH PREPARATION
Mix egg white and water together until well blended. Using a pastry brush, brush egg mixture on the top pie crust. Dust the top of the crust with 1~2 teaspoonfuls of sugar. Bake according to recipe instructions.

The egg and water mixture brushed on top helps the sugar stick to the crust as well as making the pie look shiny.

Pumpkin's Pie SERVES 16 TO 18

Thanksgiving would not be Thanksgiving in our home without the pumpkin pie. If you happen to have fresh pumpkin on hand, I say, the fresher the better.

INGREDIENTS

1 recipe .... Perfect Olive Oil Pie Crust
(see page 130)
2 tablespoons ...... pure olive oil
¾ cup.................. brown sugar
¾ cup.................. granulated sugar
1½ tablespoons ... all purpose flour
1 teaspoon........... cinnamon
¼ teaspoon.......... nutmeg
¼ teaspoon.......... cloves
½ teaspoon.......... ground ginger
2 large .... eggs
1 large .... egg white
1 can.................... low fat evaporated milk
1 large .... can pumpkin puree
1 teaspoon........... pure vanilla extract

PREPARATION

1. Preheat oven to 425°F. Prepare perfect olive oil pie crust and place in 2 pie pans. Pinch ends with the thumb between the first and second fingers.

2. In mixer bowl add olive oil, sugars, flour, cinnamon, nutmeg, cloves, and ginger. Blend until mixed.

3. Add eggs and egg white. Blend on high speed for 1 minute. Reduce mixer to low speed and gradually add evaporated milk. Mix until well blended.

4. Add pumpkin and vanilla. Mix again until blended. Pour into prepared unbaked olive oil pie shells.

5. Bake for 10 minutes. Reduce temperature to 350° F. and without opening oven door, bake for an additional 50~60 minutes or until a knife inserted into the center comes out clean.

6. Cool for 2~3 hours. If you like your pumpkin pie cold, store in the refrigerator until ready to serve.

A dollop of whipped cream always compliments a great pumpkin pie.

Sweet Apple Berry Pie Serves 8 to 10

I just love berries and this pie is packed with them. Adding a little bit of apple made it a wonderful combination of flavors and texture. All you need to complete this is to have it a la mode.

INGREDIENTS

1 recipe .... Perfect Olive Oil Pie Crust
(see page 130)
2 cups .... fresh or frozen blackberries
2 cups .... fresh or frozen blueberries
1 medium .... apple, peeled and chopped
½ cup .... brown sugar, packed
½ cup .... granulated sugar
2 tablespoons ...... fresh lemon juice
1 teaspoon .... pure vanilla extract
6 tablespoons ...... all purpose flour
1-2 tablespoons ... pure olive oil

PREPARATION

1. Preheat oven to 350°F. Prepare olive oil pie crust.

2. In a mixing bowl add blackberries. blueberries, apple, sugars, lemon juice, vanilla, and flour. Mix until well blended.

3. Pour mixture into prepared pie shell. Drizzle a tablespoon of olive oil over fruit mixture.

4. Assemble top crust and pinch edges together to seal. Slice small holes in the crust for ventilation.

5. Brush with egg wash (see page 130) and sprinkle with sugar. Place pie plate onto a large cookie sheet to catch any running juices.

6. Bake for 1 hour or until pie filling is bubbling hot. Cool for 15~30 minutes.

A Love Greater Than Pie   When my Mom and Dad were dating, my Dad happened to mention that he loved his mother's homemade strawberry pie. My Mom, wanting to win his heart, of course, and thinking 'How hard could it be?', whipped up a strawberry pie, even though she had never made one before. She used a ready-made crust and cooked it, then filled the pie crust with strawberry jam. You can imagine my Dad's face when she proudly brought it out for dessert. Because he was madly in love with her, he ate every bite. They have now been married more than 30 years and to this day, he has never told her that was not exactly how his mother, or anyone else, makes a strawberry pie.

—Robin

Triple Berry Crisp SERVES 8 TO 10

Half crisp, half cobbler. Enjoy!

INGREDIENTS

1 cup.................... fresh or frozen blueberries
1 cup.................... fresh or frozen blackberries
1 cup.................... fresh or frozen raspberries
1 cup.................... brown sugar, divided
1 cup.................... flour
½ teaspoon.......... salt
½ cup.................. quick oats
½ cup.................. buttermilk
2 teaspoons .... pure vanilla extract
⅔ cup .... pure olive oil
¼ cup.................. granulated sugar

PREPARATION

1. Preheat oven to 375°F. Coat an 8x8-inch pan with olive oil cooking spray.

2. In mixing bowl, combine all cups of three berries and ½ cup of the brown sugar. Let stand for 10 minutes.

3. In a separate mixing bowl add flour, salt, oats, the remaining brown sugar, buttermilk, vanilla, and olive oil. Mix well (by hand) to make a thick batter. Pour batter into prepared pan and spread out.

4. Spoon fruit mixture over batter and sprinkle ¼ cup sugar on top.

5. Bake 45~50 minutes or until crust is light brown and puffy. Serve with frozen yogurt or vanilla ice cream.

Olive Oil Dessert Substitution Chart

Butter, Margarine or Shortening	Pure Olive Oil
1 teaspoon	¾ teaspoon
1 tablespoon	2 teaspoons
2 tablespoons	1⅓ tablespoons
¼ cup	3 tablespoons
⅓ cup	¼ cup
½ cup	¼ cup + 1 tablespoon
⅔ cup	⅓ ~ ½ cup
¾ cup	½ cup + 1 tablespoon
1 cup	⅔ ~ ¾ cup

This chart shows approximate substitutions. When translating your favorite dessert recipes into a healthier version, you may need to use a little more or a little less heart healthy olive oil. Enjoy experimenting!

Milk Substitutes for Olive Oil Dessert Recipes

For those who have milk allergies or are lactose intolerant, listed below is a simple guide to substitute a lactose-free option in place of milk.

Tip: When shopping for lactose-free products, always read labels carefully. Some store-bought "lactose-free" products may contain small amounts of lactose.

MILK SUBSTITUTIONS
Soymilk (vanilla flavor is best)
Rice milk
Oat milk
Lactose-free milk
Almond milk

EVAPORATED MILK SUBSTITUTIONS
1. When using a lactose-free milk or soymilk, use double the amount needed of milk or soymilk. Place in a saucepan. Heat on high until it reaches a soft boil. Lower heat to medium-low and simmer until liquid is reduced to half the amount you started with.

Example: Begin with 3 cups lactose-free milk. Heat and simmer until reduced to 1½ cups.

Again, in using soymilk, vanilla flavored is best.

2. When a powdered substitute base, use 1 cup of soy powder or non dairy creamer, add ½ cup of water, soymilk, or lactose-free milk. With a blender, mix powder with liquid. Set aside for 30 minutes to thicken. Mix by hand and use in any recipe which calls for evaporated canned milk.

BUTTERMILK SUBSTITUTION
When using lactose-free milk or soymilk, for every one cup of milk add 1 tablespoon fresh lemon juice, or 1 tablespoon vinegar. I love balsamic vinegar.

Place milk in a measuring cup. Add lemon or vinegar. Stir until mixed well. Let stand for 10 minutes. Use this in your recipe as you would buttermilk.

YOGURT SUBSTITUTION
Use a soy based yogurt, often available at local grocery or health food stores.

CREAM CHEESE SUBSTITUTION
Most health food stores carry a variety of soy products. They even have a pretty good soy based cream cheese.

Egg Substitutes for Olive Oil Dessert Recipes

The cholesterol in an egg is mostly contained within the yolk. You can reduce cholesterol intake and still enjoy eggs by replacing two whole eggs with one whole egg and the whites of two eggs.

To cut cholesterol even more, try my homemade egg substitutions in place of whole eggs. When a recipe calls for egg whites, simply use them as instructed.

Generally ¼ cup egg mixture = 1 large egg

Homemade egg substitute recipe #1
6 egg whites
¼ cup nonfat dry milk
1 tablespoon extra virgin olive oil (pure or light are fine as well)

Mix all ingredients together until very well blended.
May be frozen or stored in the refrigerator for up to one week.

Homemade egg substitute recipe #2
3 egg whites
¼ cup of low-fat milk
1 tablespoon dry milk powder
1 tablespoon extra virgin olive oil (pure or light are fine as well)

Beat the egg whites lightly with a fork in a small bowl. Add the milk, powdered milk and olive oil. Beat everything until thoroughly blended. Cover and refrigerate.

Homemade egg substitute recipe #3 (lactose free)

3 egg whites
¼ cup plain soymilk or lactose-free milk
1 tablespoon ground flax seeds
1 tablespoon extra virgin olive oil (pure or light are fine as well)

Mix all ingredients together until very well blended.
May be stored in the refrigerator for up to one week.

When using egg substitutes from your local grocery store, follow package instructions.

Olive Oil Baking
Ingredients Glossary

ALL BRAN CEREAL
A cereal made from the outer layers of the wheat grain.

ALMOND EXTRACT
Flavoring made from almonds macerated in alcohol.

APPLE JUICE
Fresh or frozen juice from apples.

APPLESAUCE
Cooked, mashed apples. Sometimes a little sugar is added.

BAKING POWDER
Leavener containing baking soda, cream of tartar and cornstarch used in baking.

BAKING SODA
Bicarbonate of soda is its real name. Used to make the dough rise during baking.

BRAN FLAKES, 40%
A cereal in which 40% of its content is bran. Also featured in a Life magazine ad in 1939.

BROWN SUGAR
White sugar combined with molasses.

BUTTER
A dairy product made by churning fresh cream or milk until it coagulates.

BUTTER EXTRACT
Concentrated butter flavoring (non butter product).

BUTTERMILK
Has a slightly sour taste. It's what's left over after churning cream into butter and removing the coagulation.

CAKE FLOUR
Finely milled, low protein pastry flour.

CARROTS
A root vegetable, usually orange or white in color with a woody texture. The edible part of a carrot is a taproot. Favorite food of Bugs Bunny.

CHOCOLATE CANDY BAR
A candy bar made with: White, Milk, Semi-sweet, or Dark Chocolate. Sometimes they even put fun stuff in like coconut, nuts, caramel, or toffee!

CHOCOLATE KISSES
Little individual chocolates, wrapped in foil, with a curved tip on the end. Another reason to be happy!

CINNAMON

Strong sweet spice from the inner bark of a tropical evergreen tree.

CLOVES

Strong spice made from the dried, unopened flower bud of evergreen clove tree.

COCOA POWDER

The fruit of the cocoa plant. These beans are fermented, dried, roasted, cracked, and ground. (See Dutch Milled Cocoa Powder.)

COOKIE SCOOP

A cookie scoop looks like a mini ice cream scoop. They usually come in small, medium, and large sizes. Cookie scoops can be found at specialty kitchen shops.

CORN FLAKES

A cereal made from corn grain.

CORN SYRUP

Syrup made from cornstarch with the chemical formula $C_6H_{12}O_6$. Used in desserts, frostings, and candies.

CORNSTARCH

The starch from the maize grain, commonly known as corn.

CRAISINS

Raisin-like (sun dried) cranberries. Cranberries are a super food.

CREAM OF TARTAR

Potassium bitartrate or potassium hydrogen tartrate has the chemical formula $KC_4H_5O_6$ and is a by product of wine making. It is a potassium acid salt of tartaric acid in the form of a fine white powder and used as a stabilizer in cooking. Not related to tartar sauce.

CRISPY RICE CEREAL

A cereal made from rice and made by popping it like popcorn.

DARK CANDY BAR

Chocolate candy bar with a high content of cocoa.

DRIED BLUEBERRIES

Raisin-like (sun dried) blueberries, found in grocery and health food stores. Not to be confused with freeze dried blueberries, or frozen blueberries. Blueberries are a super food.

DUTCH MILLED COCOA POWDER

A European-milled cocoa powder that is dark in color and flavor with high cocoa content.

EGG

What comes first, the chicken or the egg?

EGG WHITE

The white part on the inside of the egg.

EGG YOLK

The yellow part on the inside of the egg.

EVAPORATED MILK

An unsweetened canned milk with about 60% of the water removed.

FLAKED COCONUT
Packaged coconut that has been sweetened and shredded.

FLOUR
There are many types of flour. In this case we are referring primarily to all purpose flour.

FRESH LEMON JUICE
Juice that is squeezed from a fresh lemon.

FRESH ORANGE JUICE
Juice that is squeezed from a fresh orange.

FROZEN BLACKBERRIES
Blackberries that have been frozen.

FROZEN BLUEBERRIES
Blueberries that have been frozen.

FROZEN RASPBERRIES
Raspberries that have been frozen.

FUJI APPLES
Developed by growers at the Tohoku Research Station in Morioka, Japan in the late 1930's and brought to market in 1962. It is a cross between the two American apple varieties, the Red Delicious and old Virginia Ralls Genet apples.

GINGER
Pungent rhizome of the common ginger plant. Often used in Asian cooking. Fresh ginger can be found in the produce aisle of your local grocery store. It is very powerful and adds a beautiful flavor to desserts. To prepare, peel off a small amount of skin and finely slice, chop or grate.

GRAHAM CRACKERS
Graham bread was invented by Sylvester Graham for his vegetarian diet. The Graham bread was high in fiber, made with non-sifted whole wheat flour and was made into little squares we now know as graham crackers.

GRANNY SMITH APPLES
Originating in Australia around 1865 from a chance seedling propagated by Marie Ana (Granny) Smith. It is thought to be a seed from malus sylvestris, the European Wild Apple, with the domestic apple M. If this origin is true, that means that this apple is a hybrid.

GRANULATED SUGAR
The term granulated sugar, meaning "sugar in granules," is often used to describe ordinary table sugar or as commonly termed, white sugar.

HONEY
The yellow stuff that comes from bees. Otherwise known as bee barf.

IODIZED SALT
Table salt to which iodine has been added.

JELLYROLL PAN
Jelly roll pan is a shallow rectangular metal pan that is 1 inch in height. Examples of pans include:

10 1/2 x 15 1/2 x 1: 10 cups
12 1/2 x 17 1/2 x 1: 12 cups

27 x 39 x 2.5cm: 2.4 liters
32 x 44 x 2.5 cm: 2.8 liters

LEMON ZEST

The outer part of the lemon skin (yellow part of the peel only), that is shaved or grated.

LIGHT CORN SYRUP

Syrup made from corn sugar.

LIGHT CREAM CHEESE

Light cream cheese (also known as Neufchatel) is a lower fat cream cheese.

MACADAMIA NUT

A white nut with a coconut-like flavor. It is used mostly in sweets. Another name for it: the Queensland Nut.

MARSHMALLOWS

The first marshmallow came out of Egypt, from the mallow root. However, they are now made from sugar, water, vanilla and gelatin. A high compression method called "jet puffing" makes the commercial varieties light and fluffy.

MERINGUE

Egg whites beaten until they are stiff, with added sugar or sugar syrup, used as a topping or shaped and baked until stiff.

MILK

A white nutritious liquid secreted by mammals and used as food by human beings. Moo.

MIXER BOWL

A mixer bowl is attached to a powerful mixer (usually 400 W or higher).

MIXING BOWL

A bowl that is usually small, medium or large. They can be glass, plastic, or metal. Mixing bowls are used to mix with by hand or with a hand mixer.

MOLASSES

Thick brown syrup separated from raw sugar during the refinement process.

NUTMEG

Pleasant spice, similar to cloves.

ORANGE ZEST

The same as Lemon Zest, only it's an orange.

PEACHES

Fruit that grows on a peach tree.

PEANUT BUTTER

Smashed peanuts mixed with salt. Look for peanut butter without hydrogenated oil.

PECANS

Pecan nuts are grown on a pecan tree, and the pecan tree is the official Texas State Tree.

PINEAPPLE JUICE

The juice from a pineapple. A pineapple is a sweet, yellow-fleshed fruit with a distinctive pinecone shape that is covered by a thick, prickly peel.

POPPY SEEDS

Small grey seed of a poppy flower; used whole or ground in baked items.

POWDERED SUGAR

Also known as confectioner's

or icing sugar that is ground into a fine powder.

PURE OLIVE OIL
See the beginning of the book!

PURE MAPLE SYRUP
A syrup made by boiling the sap of the maple tree. When boiled long enough, it becomes maple sugar. Our friends up north are famous for this stuff.

PURE VANILLA EXTRACT
Pure vanilla extract contain 13.35 ounces of vanilla beans per gallon of liquid and contains 35% alcohol.

QUICK OATS (OATMEAL)
Quick oats are oat groats (Oats of Oatmeal) that have been cut into pieces and rolled even finer to cook faster; about 5 minutes. (Anyway, it got me a "Q" entry in the Glossary.)

RAISINS
Raisins are dried grapes. Raisins can be eaten raw or used in cooking and baking.

SALT
Sodium chloride, also known as common salt, table salt, or halite, is a chemical compound with the formula $NaCl$. Sodium chloride is the salt most responsible for the salinity of the ocean and of the extra-cellular fluid of many multi-cellular organisms. As the main ingredient in edible salt, it is commonly used as a condiment and food preservative and can be found in the Great Salt Lake. Was that more than you wanted to know?

SEMI SWEET CHOCOLATE CHIPS
Semi-Sweet Chocolate Chips are a carefully balanced blend of the finest ingredients, including real cocoa butter, unsweetened chocolate, and sugar.

SOFT PEAKS
Regarding egg whites. While beating egg whites at a high speed, air mixes until the whites form soft peaks. The peaks will curl over and droop.

STIFF PEAKS
Stiff peaks stand straight up. As with meringue.

STRAWBERRY JAM
Smashed strawberries cooked with pectin and sugar.

TART APPLES
Granny Smith apples are pretty tart. There really was a Granny Smith. Maria Anna Sherwood Smith, Australia 1865.

TOFFEE CHIPS
Tiny pieces of hard toffee candy.

UNSWEETENED CHOCOLATE BAKING SQUARES
Unsweetened chocolate designed for baking. It is kept in the baking aisle.

VANILLA BAKING CHIPS
They look just like chocolate chips, only they are white and made with vanilla.

VANILLA BEAN ICE CREAM

The most moist and flavorful beans come from the plants that are grown in the tropical climates of Tahiti and Madagascar. Vanilla beans have been used as a flavoring for hundreds of years, and it seems so fitting that such an extraordinarily pleasing flavor would come from the fruit of a climbing Orchid Vine! All that put into ice cream.

VANILLA PUDDING MIX

Dry, instant pudding mix is best.

VANILLA YOGURT

Made by fermenting partly skim or skim milk with a special live culture and adding vanilla flavoring. It is custard like in texture.

WALNUTS

Genus Juglans. Nuts from the walnut tree.

WATER

If you needed to look this one up, e-mail me and I'll sign you up for one of my cooking classes.

WHITE CHOCOLATE

A blend of sugar, cocoa butter, milk solids, lecithin and vanilla.

WIRE RACKS

Racks made out of wire. Usually used to cool baked goods. They are elevated, therefore leaving room for air to flow around your goodie. Can be found in any cooking store.

YEAST

Leavening agent. Used for fermenting dough in making breads, rolls, and anything else you want to be big and fluffy!!

Baking Definitions

BAKE

To cook in the oven. Food is cooked slowly with gentle heat, causing the natural moisture to evaporate slowly, concentrating the flavor.

BATTER

A mixture of flour, fat, and liquid that is thin enough in consistency to require a pan to encase it. Used in such preparations as cakes and some cookies. A batter is different from dough, which maintains its shape.

BEAT

To smooth a mixture by briskly whipping or stirring it with a spoon, fork, wire whisk, rotary beater, or electric mixer.

BIND

To thicken a sauce or hot liquid by stirring in ingredients such as eggs, flour, butter, or cream.

BLEND

To mix or fold two or more ingredients together to obtain equal distribution throughout the mixture.

BROWN

A quick sautéing, pan/oven broiling, or grilling method done either at the beginning or end of meal preparation, often to enhance flavor, texture, or eye appeal.

BRUSH

Using a pastry brush, to coat a food such as meat or bread with melted butter, glaze, or other liquid.

BUNDT PAN

The generic name for any tube baking pan having fluted sides (though it was once a trademarked name).

CARAMELIZATION

Browning sugar over a flame, with or without the addition of some water to aid the process. The temperature range in which sugar caramelizes is approximately 320°F to 360°F (160°C to 182°C).

COAT

To evenly cover a pan or baking dish.

COMBINE

To blend two or more ingredients into a single mixture.

CORE

To remove the inedible center of fruits such as apples and pears.

CREAM

To quickly mix moist ingredients together until smooth. This usually involves sugar.

CRIMP

To create a decorative edge on a piecrust. On a double pie crust, this also seals the edges together.

CRISP

To restore the crunch to foods. Vegetables such as celery and carrots can be crisped with an ice water bath, and foods such as stale crackers can be heated in a medium oven.

CRUSH

To condense a food to its smallest particles, usually using a mortar and pestle or a rolling pin. Also a word my twelve year old son uses to describe his feelings about the young lady he adores this week.

CRYSTALLIZE

To form sugar- or honey-based syrups into crystals. The term also describes the coating.

CURD

Custard-like pie or tart filling flavored with juice and zest of citrus fruit, usually lemon, although lime and orange may also be used. Also, something Miss Muffet likes to eat.

CUSTARD

A mixture of beaten egg, milk, and possibly other ingredients such as sweet or savory flavorings, which is cooked with gentle heat, often in a water bath or double boiler. As pie filling, the custard is frequently cooked and chilled before being layered into a pre-baked crust.

CUT IN
To work olive oil into dry ingredients.

DASH
A measurement approximately equal to 1/16 teaspoon, or to move with haste.

DOT
To sprinkle food with small bits of an ingredient such as butter to allow for even melting.

DOUGH
A combination of ingredients including flour, water or milk, and, sometimes, a leavener, producing a firm but workable mixture for making baked goods.

DREDGE
To sprinkle lightly and evenly with sugar or flour. A dredger has holes pierced on the lid to sprinkle evenly.

DRIZZLE
To pour a liquid such as a sweet glaze in a slow, light trickle over food.

DUST
To sprinkle food lightly with spices, sugar, or flour for a light coating.

EGG WASH
A mixture of beaten eggs (yolks, whites, or whole eggs) with either milk or water. Used to coat cookies and other baked goods to give them a shine when baked.

FOLD
To cut and mix lightly with a spoon to keep as much air in the mixture as possible.

FRITTER
Sweet or savory foods coated or mixed into batter, then deep fried (also, in French, beignet).

FRY
To cook food in hot cooking oil, usually until a crisp brown crust forms.

GANACHE
A rich chocolate filling or coating made with chocolate, vegetable shortening, and possibly heavy cream. It can coat cakes or cookies, and can be used as a filling for truffles.

GARNISH
A decorative piece of an edible ingredient such as parsley, lemon wedges, croutons, or chocolate curls placed as a finishing touch to dishes or drinks.

GLAZE
A liquid that gives an item a shiny surface. Examples are fruit jams that have been heated or chocolate thinned with olive oil. Also, to cover a food with such a liquid.

GLUTEN
A protein formed when hard wheat flour is moistened and agitated. Gluten is what gives yeast dough its characteristic elasticity.

GRATE

To shred or cut down a food into fine pieces by rubbing it against a grated surface.

GREASE

To coat a pan or skillet with a thin layer of oil or non-stick cooking spray.

GRIND

To mechanically cut a food into small pieces.

HARD-BALL STAGE

In candy making, the point at which syrup has cooked long enough to form a solid ball in cold water. Approximately 250°~265°F.

HULL (ALSO HUSK)

To remove the leafy parts of soft fruits, such as strawberries or blackberries (or corn).

ICE

(1) To cool down cooked food by placing in ice; (2) to spread frosting on a cake.

INFUSION

Extracting flavors by soaking them in liquid heated in a covered pan. The term also refers to the liquid resulting from this process.

JULIENNE

To cut into long, thin strips.

KNEAD

To work dough with the heels of your hands in a pressing and folding motion until it becomes smooth and elastic.

LEAVENER

An ingredient or process that produces air bubbles and causes the rising of baked goods such as cookies and cakes.

LINE

To place layers of edible (cake or bread slices) or inedible (foil or wax paper) ingredients in a pan to provide structure for a dish or to prevent sticking.

MARBLE

To gently swirl one food into another.

MERINGUE

Egg whites beaten until they are stiff, then sweetened. Meringue can be used as the topping for pies, or baked as cookies.

MINCE

To chop food into tiny, irregular pieces.

MIX

To beat or stir two or more foods together until they are thoroughly combined.

MOISTEN

Adding enough liquid to dry ingredients to dampen but not soak them.

PARCHMENT

A heavy, heat-resistant paper used in cooking.

PEAKS

The mounds made in a mixture. For example, egg white that has been whipped to stiffness. Peaks are "stiff" if they stay upright, or "soft" if they curl over. Also the top of a mountain.

PINCH

Same as "dash."

PIZZA CUTTER

Circular blade mounted as a wheel on a handle, used to cut pizza.

PROOF

To let yeast dough rise.

RAMEKIN

A small baking dish used for individual servings of sweet and savory dishes.

SCALD

Cooking a liquid such as milk to just below the point of boiling.

SCORE

To make a number of shallow (often diagonal) cuts across a surface.

SET

Let food rest undisturbed until firm.

SIFT

To remove large lumps from a dry ingredient such as flour or confectioner's sugar by passing it through a fine mesh colander. This process also incorporates air into the ingredients, making them lighter.

SIMMER

Cooking food in a liquid at a low enough temperature that small bubbles begin to break the surface.

SKIM

To remove the top fat layer from stocks, soups, sauces, or other liquids such as cream from milk.

SPRINGFORM PAN

A two-part baking pan in which a spring-loaded collar fits around a base; the collar is removed after baking is complete. Used for foods that may be difficult to remove from regular pans, such as cheesecake.

THIN

To reduce a mixture's thickness with the addition of more liquid.

TOSS

To thoroughly combine several ingredients by mixing lightly.

UNLEAVENED

Baked goods that contain no agents to give them volume, such as baking powder, baking soda, or yeast.

WHIP

To incorporate air into ingredients such as cream or egg whites by beating until light and fluffy; also refers to the utensil used for this action.

WHISK

To mix or fluff by beating; also refers to the utensil used for this action.

ZEST

The thin, brightly colored outer part of the rind of citrus fruits. It contains volatile oils, used as a flavoring.

MEDICAL BENEFITS OF OLIVE OIL ENDNOTES

[1] Penny Kris-Etherton, PhD, RD; Robert H. Eckel, MD; Barbara V. Howard, PhD; Sachiko St. Jeor, PhD, RD; Terry L. Bazzarre, PhD, "Lyon Diet Heart Study: Benefits of a Mediterranean-Style, National Cholesterol Education Program/American Heart Association Step I Dietary Pattern on Cardiovascular Disease", 2001, <http://circ.ahajournals.org/cgi/content/full/103/13/1823>, (22 February 2007).

[2] Amy Murphy, "Blood vessels appear healthier after people consume olive oil high in phenolic compounds", 11 November 2005, <http://www.medicalnewstoday.com/medicalnews.php?newsid=33381>, (22 February 2007).

[3] "FDA Allows Qualified Health Claim to Decrease Risk of Coronary Heart Disease", 1 November 2004, <http://www.fda.gov/bbs/topics/news/2004/NEW01129.html>, (22 February 2007).

[4] "Olive Oil reduces blood pressure", 4 November 2004, <http://ww.nutraingredients.com/news/news-NG.asp?n=55854-olive-oil-reduces>, (22 February 2007).

[5] "Olive oil linked to lower blood pressure", 8 January 2007, <http://www.nutraingredients-usa.com/news/ng.asp?id=73151-olive-oil-mediterranean-diet-blood-pressure>, (22 February 2007).

[6] L. Aldo Ferrara, MD; A. Sonia Raimondi, MD; Lucia d'Episcopo, RD; Luci Guida, MD; Antonia Dello Russo, MS; Teodoro Marotta, MD, PhD, "Olive Oil and Reduced Need for Antihypertensive Medications", 27 March 2000, <http://archinte.ama-assn.org/cgi/content/abstract/160/6/837>, (23 February 2007).

[7] María-Isabel Covas, MSc, PhD; Kristiina Nyyssönen, MSc, PhD; Henrik E. Poulsen, MD, PhD; Jari Kaikkonen, MSc, PhD; Hans-Joachim F. Zunft, MD, PhD; Holger Kiesewetter, MD, PhD; Antonio Gaddi, MD, PhD; Rafael de la Torre, MSc, PhD; Jaakko Mursu, MSc; Hans Bäumler, MSc, PhD; Simona Nascetti, MD, PhD; Jukka T. Salonen, MD, PhD; Montserrat Fitó, MD, PhD; Jyrki Virtanen, MSc; Jaume Marrugat, MD, PhD, "The Effect of Polyphenols in Olive Oil on Heart Disease Risk Factors", 5 September 2006, <http://www.annals.org/cgi/content/abstract/145/5/333#FN>, (23 February 2007).

[8] "Why does Mediterranean diet protect women from breast cancer" It's in the olive oil", 10 January 2005, <http://www.medicalnewstoday.com/medicalnews.php?newsid=18751>, (23 February 2007).
J.A. Menendez, L. Vellon, R. Colomer, & R. Lupu, "Oleic acid, the main monounsaturated fatty acid of olive oil, suppresses Her-2/*neu* (*erb* B-2) expression and synergistically enhances the growth

inhibitory effects of trastuzumab (Herceptin™) in breast cancer cells with Her-2/*neu* oncogene amplification", 10 January 2005, <http://annonc.oxfordjournals.org/cgi/reprint/mdi090v1.pdf>, (23 February 2007).

[9] Roberto Fabiani, Angelo De Bartolomeo, Patrizia Rosignoli, Maurizio Servili, Roberto Selvaggini, Gian Francesco Montedoro, Cristina Di Saverio and Guido Morozzi, March 2006, "Virgin Olive Oil Phenols Inhibit Proliferation of Human Promyelocytic Leukemia Cells (HL60) by Inducing Apoptosis and Differentiation", <http://jn.nutrition.org/cgi/content/abstract/136/3/614>, (23 February 2007).

[10] "Prevent Cancer, Use Olive Oil: New Year's Resolution No. 1", 24 December 2006, <http://www.medicalnewstoday.com/medicalnews.php?newsid=58759>, (23 February 2007).
Anja Machowetz, Henrik E. Poulsen, Sindy Gruendel, Allan Weimann, Montserrat Fitó, Jaume Marrugat, Rafael de la Torre, Jukka T. Salonen, Kristiina Nyyssönen, Jaakko Mursu, Simona Nascetti, Antonio Gaddi, Holger Kiesewetter, Hans Bäumler, Hany Selmi, Jari Kaikkonen, Hans-Joachim F. Zunft, Maria-Isabel Covas and Corinna Koebnick, "Effect of olive oils on biomarkers of oxidative DNA stress in Northern and Southern Europeans" January 2007, <http://www.fasebj.org/cgi/content/abstract/21/1/45>, (23 February 2007).

[11] L Sköldstam, L Hagfors, G Johansson, "An experimental study of a Mediterranean diet intervention for patients with rheumatoid arthritis", 28 June 2002, <http://ard.bmj.com/cgi/content/full/62/3/208>, (22 February 2007).

I want to have a good body, but not as much as I want dessert.

Jason Love

Index